MARCUS AURELIUS

Meditations: Uncensored and Unleashed

Contents

Notes from the Translator

Meditations is not a lecture, nor a self-help guide, nor a philosophical treatise. It was likely never intended for anyone other than the author. It is not a "meditation" in the sense of Buddhism, Hinduism, or any Eastern Philosophy. *Meditations* is the author's record of thoughts to himself: a very personal philosophical exercise in Stoicism, both for the author and for anyone reading it. While reading *Meditations*, it is important to constantly remind ourselves that the author is not lecturing us, the readers; he is writing to himself.

Much like *Meditations*, this book was a personal project that I initially never intended to publish. It was a project to satisfy my own curiosity. After some reflection on the countless hours that I spent on this project, I decided to publish something that I consider to be an incomplete and imperfect work, thinking that there may be someone out there in the Cosmos who would find it interesting, useful, or maybe even entertaining. This book is the result of my journey *down a rabbit hole.* It was a side-project that I started because I was curious to see if I could get as close to the most original essence of *Meditations* as possible.

I started reading *Meditations* many years ago. The tone of the versions I read was either academic or Victorian. The message always resonated with me, but there was something about the tone that bothered me. As I learned more about the Roman Empire over the years, I had a nagging suspicion that there was something not quite right about the translations I had read; many translations of Meditations seemed, in some passages, to differ wildly.

Meditations resonated with me as an adolescent. Here was the Emperor of Rome, one of the most powerful people in the world at the time of the writing, yet he struggled to understand his own existence and purpose. Here was a man confronting his mortality, trying to make sense of the world. I was a young person looking forward; Marcus was an old man looking back. We were doing the same thing.

In the process of conceptualizing this book, it became clear to me that Marcus had been a mentor to me across a gap of almost twenty centuries. My conduct in life, both personally and professionally, loosely followed Stoic philosophy, though I never recognized how deeply I had learned from Marcus.

A number of years ago, I obtained an older translation of *Meditations* (George Long, 1862) and started a different project. The wording made parts of it tedious to read, and the tone of Marcus, in places, was that of a 19th-century English gentleman. Using simple search and replace of modern computer text editors, I started to modernize the language of the text, and the result was something that was more readable, but clearly translated and adapted to the sensibilities of the era in which it was translated.

I was not satisfied with the results of that exercise. Long did make an effort to be true to the Greek where possible, and translated lines and words, such as passages mentioning slavery, that even modern translators tiptoe around. That abandoned project to "modernize" the 1862 translation was not a waste of time and effort; it opened my eyes to the fact that what I had been reading over the years may not have been the pure essence of the original writing, as much as such a thing is possible today.

All I had accomplished with that exercise was to render a more palatable version of a Victorian-era translation for the modern reader, basically converting all the "thee," "thou," and "thy" to modern equivalents. A more readable version of existing Victorian-era translations was not my goal. What I truly wanted was a version that reflected what Marcus actually wrote and clearly dealt with the Stoic concepts. Something that captured the essence, culture, and biases of the time in which it was written, during the apex of the Roman Empire.

Very recently, after some research, I discovered the Wilhelm Xylander *editio princeps*: a 16th-century Latin translation of *Meditations*, published alongside a copy of the original Greek text. The Xylander texts were fascinating, as they were copied and translated from a manuscript known as the *Codex Palatinus* (P; also designated *Codex Toxitanus*, T).

It was clear that if I ever wanted to read the purest and uncensored version of *Meditations* available, then I would need to start with the Xylander texts.

At the end of last year (2025), I set to work, first downloading the approximately 490 pages of scanned material, then, with the help of modern optical character recognition (OCR), converting the material to Latin and Greek text.

Upon spot-checking the original Xylander Latin and the Greek text printed by Andreas Gessner, I confirmed my suspicions: modern translations that I had been reading most of my life had indeed been censored, softened, or paraphrased.

I started out with the Latin translation. I worked page by page to stitch together the translations and end up with the full text of each book. I concentrated first on the Latin texts and then I moved on to the Greek texts. When I was satisfied that I had both Greek and Latin texts in plain text format, I set to work translating to English.

Now, here is where things get interesting. Latin grammar is somewhat closer to modern English than Koine Greek. I was able to get some very coherent translations directly from the Latin text. Koine Greek, on the other hand, is a completely different beast. The results of the direct literal translations from Koine Greek to English yielded text that was, at best, a challenge to comprehend, and at worst, something that was barely intelligible to a modern English reader. After a while of reading the Greek translations, the grammar and word order reminded me of the speech patterns of the fictional character Yoda.

At first, I wanted to prefer the Latin translations, as the text seemed more readable versus the Greek translations. However, after comparing some of the Latin translations to the Greek, it became apparent that the Latin translation was just that: another translation. I decided that I needed to work with the Koine Greek as much as possible if I wanted to accomplish my objective. The details of my three-source approach and the rationale behind it are discussed in "On the Xylander Texts."

I welcome corrections and will incorporate them into future editions. This has been a lifelong pursuit for me, studying multiple traditions of Philosophy from Stoicism, to the Epistemology of Kant and Metaphysics of Hegel, to the Existentialism of Kierkegaard, Nietzsche, and Sartre. I am an Information Technology professional and all-around technology enthusiast; Philosophy is a side interest. But I am accustomed to revisions of software, and have no hesitation in revising a book if I get something wrong; this book is my first published attempt to apply a methodical modern technological approach to Philosophy with a system of untranslated or capitalized Stoic words. As admitted earlier, I think this work has room to be perfected (and perhaps never will be perfect with the time I have available). I could probably spend countless hours further refining and striving toward an ideal, but that would mean that it would never be shared with another person. There are many more footnotes I would have liked to add, and many more words I would have liked to verify against my capitalization system. I set a deadline for myself to publish, and that deadline has passed.

So here is the book, as it is. This may not be the most traditionally precise translation of the Meditations, but I hope it better captures the tone and perspective in which it was originally written: an aging emperor's private notes to himself, in a violent and uncertain world, confronting his own mortality and trying to make sense of the Cosmos. I leave it to the reader to judge whether I succeeded.

In my opinion, humanity needs Philosophy now more than ever.

Patrick Tiquet, February 2026

Uncensored and Unleashed

At some point during the process of translating the Xylander Greek, I started to realize that this book might need an "Explicit Content Advisory" label on the cover.

I am joking. Mostly.

When I started this project, I suspected that existing translations had softened or sanitized Marcus's writing. What I did not fully expect was just how raw the original Greek text actually is. The *Meditations* that most English readers know is a dignified, contemplative work of philosophy. The *Meditations* that Marcus actually wrote is that too, but it is also blunt, crude, and at times shockingly graphic. He was writing to himself, in private, with no expectation that anyone would ever read these notebooks. He was not trying to impress an audience. He was trying to hold himself together, and stripping Impressions down to their bare reality.

Once I began working directly from the Greek, I kept encountering passages where the originals were far more visceral than anything I had seen in the translations I had read over the years. Passages that had been quietly omitted, softened into vagueness, or paraphrased into something respectable. What follows are some representative examples of what I found, and what this translation preserves. I should note that many such passages are also preserved in the modern Greek in some form and are not universally unique to the Xylander texts. However, many translations available in English today often omit, soften, or overly paraphrase many of these passages.

The body as gore. In 2.2, Marcus describes himself in terms that would not be out of place in a medical dissection:

"Whatever this is that I am, it is a little flesh, a little Pneuma, and the

Ruling Faculty... despise the flesh: it is gore, and small bones, and a little woven network of nerves, veins, and arteries."

Most translations render this more delicately. Marcus did not write delicately. He was deliberately stripping away the illusion of bodily dignity to remind himself that what he really is, what matters, is the Ruling Faculty.

Sexual intercourse as friction of entrails. In 6.13, Marcus performs his characteristic exercise of reducing impressive-seeming things to their bare physical components:

"...concerning sexual intercourse, that it is the friction of entrails and, with a certain spasm, the ejection of a little snot."

This is probably the passage that made me think about the advisory label. It is not obscene for the sake of being obscene. It is a Stoic philosophical exercise: strip the Impression, see the thing as it really is, and the irrational Desire falls away. But translators have consistently softened this. "The coupling of bodies" or "a convulsive motion" are typical substitutes. Marcus's Greek is far more specific and far more deliberately disgusting. He meant it to be. That was the point.

"He has nowhere to shit." In 5.12, Marcus quotes a line from comedy about a wealthy man so consumed by his possessions that, despite his abundance, he "has nowhere to shit" (οὐκ ἔχειν ὅποι χέσῃ). The Greek is plain and vulgar. Most translators either skip the line or render it as something along the lines of "he has no room to move." I have translated it as Marcus wrote it.

Erotic Passions for boys. In 1.16, Marcus praises his adoptive father Antoninus Pius for having "put a stop to the erotic Passions for boys." The Greek literally refers to the erotic loves of lads or adolescents (ἔρωτας τῶν μειρακίων). Victorian translations typically obscure this to something like "he checked widespread vice," which obscures what Marcus actually said. He was not making a general statement about public morality. He was crediting his father with ending a specific set of erotic pursuits that were commonplace in the Roman imperial court.

Discharge as the origin of life. In 10.26, Marcus reflects on the mystery of human generation with startling bluntness:

"Having discharged semen into a womb, he withdrew. Then another Cause takes over, and works and completes an infant. What a thing from such a source!"

The Greek is direct: Σπέρμα εἰς μήτραν ἀφείς ἀπεχώρησε ("Having discharged seed into a womb, he withdrew"). Other translations consistently soften this to something like "having deposited seed" or "having implanted life." Marcus's language is clinical and deliberately unrefined. He is marveling at the gap between the crudeness of the physical act and the astonishing complexity of what it produces. The philosophical point is lost if the language is prettified.

Catamites, prostitutes, and slaves. Marcus does not shy away from the realities of Roman life. In 5.10, he observes that worldly possessions are "capable of being possessed by a catamite or a prostitute" (κιναίδου ἤ πόρνης). In 6.14, he notes that some people's idea of cultivation amounts to nothing more than "the possession of a multitude of slaves," a passage that is, as I note in the footnotes, often a target of censorship, sometimes translated as "management of a great estate." In 6.34, he lists "robbers, catamites, patricides, and tyrants" in a single breath. These are not aberrations in the text. They are the texture of a Roman emperor's reality, and Marcus uses them for philosophical purposes: to illustrate the worthlessness of external goods, the corruption of those who pursue Pleasure without Reason, and the insignificance of social status.

Heraclitus, cowshit, and lice. In 3.3, Marcus catalogs the deaths of great men to drive home the universality of mortality:

"Heraclitus, after his many inquiries into the Conflagration of the Cosmos, died swollen with water and smeared with cowshit. Lice destroyed Democritus, and other lice destroyed Socrates."

The philosopher of fire, waterlogged and dung-smeared: the irony is intentional and crystal clear. And the word for "lice" (φθεῖρες) carries a double meaning in Greek: both literal vermin and metaphorical "destroyers." Marcus is being simultaneously crude and clever, which is precisely the combination that gets lost when translators clean him up.

"Yesterday a drop of mucus, tomorrow pickled flesh or ashes." In 4.48, Marcus compresses an entire human life into a single sentence. The "drop of mucus" is semen (or, at best, the fluid of conception). The "pickled flesh or ashes" refers to the two Roman treatments of the dead: embalming and cremation. It is a brutal summary, and it is entirely characteristic of Marcus at his most unflinching.

These are some representative examples of passages that have been suppressed through the centuries, whether by censorship, academic interpretation, or softening through paraphrase. Throughout this translation, wherever Marcus was graphic, vulgar, or blunt, I have let him be graphic, vulgar, and blunt. Not because I wanted to shock anyone, but because that is what he wrote. The rawness is not incidental to the philosophy. It *is* the philosophy. Stoic practice demands that we see things as they truly are, stripped of the Impressions and narratives we project onto them. Marcus practiced what he preached, starting with his own body, his own mortality, and the messy physical reality of human existence.

If that occasionally reads like a book that needs a parental advisory sticker, then perhaps that tells us something about how far other translations have drifted from the original.

On the Xylander Texts

It is largely to the credit of Wilhelm Xylander, Conrad Gessner, and Andreas Gessner[1] that we have *Meditations* at all.

The story begins with a single Greek manuscript, now known as the *Codex Palatinus* (P), which had survived through the ages in the Palatine Library at Heidelberg. Conrad Gessner, the Swiss naturalist and bibliographer, recognized the significance of this damaged manuscript and arranged for it to be published. At his urging, Wilhelm Xylander, a scholar of Greek at the University of Heidelberg, produced a Latin translation. Xylander published both his Latin translation (1558) and the Greek text (1559), in the *editio princeps*, the first printed edition of Marcus Aurelius's personal notebooks. Andreas Gessner oversaw the printing of the Greek text in Zurich. Without the efforts of these three men, it is entirely possible that the manuscript could have deteriorated beyond any point of recovery, and significant portions of *Meditations* might have been lost to the world, or the entire manuscript lost in obscurity.

Xylander himself was remarkably candid about the condition of his source material. In his dedicatory epistle to Georg von Stetten the Younger (included at the end of this book), he describes the Greek manuscript as "mutilated, wretchedly damaged, and curtailed in a great part." He admits that in places he "had to divine or departed boldly from the Greek text," and he defends publishing an imperfect edition over letting the work remain unknown. His honesty about the limitations of his own work is, to my mind, one of the most admirable things about the entire enterprise. He knew it was incomplete. He published it anyway, because an imperfect *Meditations* was better than no *Meditations* at all.

That candid acknowledgment of incompleteness is precisely what drove me to cross-reference the Xylander Greek against modern critical editions. If even Xylander considered his text to be damaged and incomplete, then I could not rely on it as a sole source. I needed to verify what was there, identify what was missing, and determine where the text had been corrupted over the centuries of transmission.

Translation Objectives

My primary objective was straightforward: to produce a translation that captures the original Roman perspective of Marcus Aurelius's private notebooks, without the layers of censorship, adjustment to contemporary theological terminology, and Victorian propriety that have accumulated over centuries of translation. I wanted the reader to encounter Marcus as he was, not as later translators wished he had been.

To accomplish this, I needed to work as close to the original Greek as possible. The Xylander Greek text served as my primary source. I referenced the Xylander Latin translation only for clarity, when the Greek was ambiguous, damaged, or otherwise difficult to parse. Where the Xylander Greek showed gaps, corruptions, or suspected errors, I turned to modern critical Greek editions of *Meditations* to fill in what was missing and to verify what was present.

This three-source approach (Xylander Greek as primary, Xylander Latin for reference, modern critical Greek for validation) allowed me to produce a translation grounded in the earliest available printed text while accounting for its known deficiencies.

The modern critical Greek text used for cross-reference throughout this translation is the edition of J. H. Leopold (Oxford Classical Texts, 1908), accessed digitally through the Perseus Digital Library at Tufts University. Where this text diverges from the Xylander Greek, the discrepancy is noted in the footnotes. Later critical editions by A. S. L. Farquharson (1944) and Joachim Dalfen (Teubner, 1979; rev. 1987) have since superseded Leopold's text in some readings; where these editions are known to differ on passages discussed in the footnotes, the discrepancy is noted.

Validating the Xylander Greek

The process of comparing the Xylander Greek against modern critical editions revealed a range of discrepancies: missing words, variant readings, and occasional corruptions that had entered the text through centuries of manuscript transmission. Some of these are minor. Others affect the meaning of the passage. A few examples from the footnotes will illustrate the kinds of issues I encountered:

In 1.16, the Xylander Greek text is missing the phrase οὐδὲ μὴν εὐπαράγωγον ὑπ' αὐτῶν ("nor was he easily led astray by them"), which appears in modern critical editions. This is a complete clause, absent from the earliest printed text, that had to be supplied from later manuscript traditions.

In 1.16, the Xylander Greek reads τελώνη (*telōnē*, "tax collector"), where modern texts read φελώνη (*phelōnē*), meaning a cloak or mantle. A single-letter difference that changes the meaning of the entire passage: Marcus is likely talking about his adoptive father's simple clothing from the country, not a tax collector, as the whole passage deals with simple clothing. I did leave the "tax-collector" reference in my translation, with a footnote explaining the discrepancy, because it was what was in the original Xylander text, and he echoes the "tax collector" in his Latin translation. Was it a cloak or was it a tax collector? Xylander certainly thought it was a "tax collector". Modern critical Greek versions seem to disagree. Such are the pitfalls of translating ancient texts.

In 2.5, the Xylander Greek reads θεοειδῆ ("God-like"), where modern consolidated Greek texts have θεουδῆ ("God-fearing"). Xylander's Latin confirms his reading: *divinae similem* ("resembling the divine"). Both readings are defensible, but they point the passage in different philosophical directions.

In 2.11, a word is omitted entirely from the Xylander Greek version. Modern texts supply "speak" in the sequence "act, speak, and think accordingly." Without it, the triad that Marcus clearly intended is incomplete.

In 4.20, the word λύρα (*lyra*, "lyre") is present in modern Greek texts but omitted from the Xylander Greek, leaving a gap in Marcus's list of things that do not need external praise to retain their worth.

In 4.33, modern translations and modern Greek sources record the name Dentatus (Manius Curius Dentatus, the legendary Roman hero), while Xylander's 1558/59 Greek copy records this as *Leonnatus* (Λεοννάτος), and his Latin translation confirms the same. This translation uses Xylander's "Leonnatus" even though it may be an error by Xylander or an earlier writer.

In 8.27, almost all modern English editions translate a key word as "vessel" or "body" (referring to the physical container surrounding us). Xylander has αἴτιον ("cause"), and his Latin translates it as *causam proximam* ("proximate cause"). This is a significant philosophical divergence: the difference between a material and a causal relationship to the Cosmos.

In 9.32, Xylander reads τὸν ἴδιον αἰῶνα ("your own lifetime"), where modern texts read τὸν ἀίδιον αἰῶνα ("everlasting Eternity"). Again, a single-letter variant that transforms the scope of Marcus's reflection from the personal to the cosmic. The Xylander reading was adopted in this translation.

In 11.26, Xylander has "Ephesians" in both Greek and Latin texts, where some manuscripts read "Epicureans" (Ἐπικουρείων). If "Epicureans" is correct, the passage attributes a specific precept to the Epicurean school; if "Ephesians," it may refer to Heraclitean traditions associated with the city of Ephesus.

These are not exhaustive examples, but they are representative. They illustrate why a translation based solely on any single source, even one as historically significant as the Xylander *editio princeps*, would be incomplete at best and misleading at worst. Every discrepancy noted in this translation is flagged in the footnotes so the reader can see exactly where the sources diverge and which reading was adopted.

It is also worth acknowledging that even the modern critical editions may not represent the complete original text. Portions of *Meditations* may have been lost forever, damaged beyond recovery before any surviving copy was made. What we have is what survived, and there is no guarantee that it is everything Marcus wrote.

Why the Xylander Greek

Every modern translation of *Meditations* available today is based on modern critical editions of the Greek text. These editions are the product of centuries of painstaking scholarship: combination of manuscript variants, cross-referencing with other ancient sources, linguistic analysis, and the accumulated judgment of generations of academics. They are, by any measure, superior texts in terms of completeness and accuracy. Words that were missing from the earliest printed text have been restored. Corruptions introduced by medieval scribes have been identified and corrected. Passages that were garbled in the manuscript have been reconstructed through comparison with parallel sources, quotations in other ancient authors, and the internal logic of Marcus's own arguments. The modern critical editions represent the best available reconstruction of what Marcus actually wrote.

So why not simply use them?

Because completeness and accuracy are not the only things that matter in a translation. The same centuries of scholarship that improved the text also changed it in ways that have nothing to do with recovering Marcus's original words. Every generation of editors brought its own assumptions, sensibilities, and biases to the text. Scholars smoothed out passages that fit uncomfortably with their theology (see my previous reference in this section regarding 2.5: "God-like" vs. "God-fearing"). Victorian editors softened language that offended their propriety. Twentieth-century academics made interpretive choices that reflected the philosophical fashions of their time. These interventions were not always conscious, and they were rarely malicious, but they were cumulative. Layer by layer, the text was adjusted, refined, and in places, domesticated.

The result is that modern critical editions, for all their scholarly rigor, carry an invisible editorial inheritance. When a modern editor chooses between two variant readings, that choice is informed not only by the manuscript evidence but by a long tradition of what we think *Meditations* is supposed to say. When a passage can be read as either blunt or restrained, the restrained reading has been preferred, again and again, for centuries. When Marcus's language is crude, or his social observations are uncomfortable for a modern audience, the tendency has been to smooth, to soften, to interpret rather than to transcribe. This is not a conspiracy. It is the natural result of a text passing through the hands of people who admired it and wanted it to be admirable on their own terms.

The Xylander Greek predates all of that. It is the *editio princeps*, the first printed Greek text of *Meditations*, published in 1558/59 from a manuscript that Xylander himself described as, to paraphrase: damaged, incomplete, and difficult to read. It has none of the benefits of modern scholarship. It is missing words. It contains errors. In places, it is almost certainly wrong.

But it also has something that no modern critical edition can offer: it is as far back into the past as we can go in printed text, untouched by centuries of translations and editorial conjecture that have occurred since it was first published in 1558/59. When Xylander printed his Greek text, there was no established interpretation of *Meditations* to conform to. There were no centuries of English translations setting expectations for what Marcus should sound like. There was no Victorian sensibility to offend, no Christian orthodoxy demanding that a pagan emperor's private notebooks align with later theological dogmas. Xylander printed what he found, damage and all, and he, in his prefatory *Dedicatory Epistle* of his *editio princeps*, even voiced his own concerns about the completeness of the work.

That is precisely what makes the Xylander text valuable as a primary source for this translation. Not because it is better than the modern critical editions, but because it is independent of them. It preserves readings that later editors emended, not always because those readings were wrong, but sometimes because they were inconvenient, unfamiliar, or philosophically unfashionable. It records the text as it existed before anyone decided what it was supposed to mean.

This independence comes to us at a real cost. There are passages where the Xylander Greek is clearly inferior to the modern critical text: words missing, names garbled, phrases that make no grammatical sense because, likely, the original manuscript was damaged or obscured in exactly that spot. I am not blind to these deficiencies, and I have not ignored them.

It is also worth considering where these errors and omissions actually came from, because the answer is not as simple as it might appear. Some were almost certainly introduced during the printing process itself; sixteenth-century typesetting of Greek was a demanding craft, and compositors working from a damaged manuscript in an unfamiliar hand would have made mistakes. Some may have entered the text earlier, through the long chain of scribal copying that transmitted *Meditations* from antiquity to the Palatine Library. A scribe working centuries before Xylander, copying by hand from an already deteriorating example, could have misread a word, skipped a line, or silently emended a passage he found confusing. And some of the irregularities may not be errors at all. Marcus was writing personal notes, private philosophical exercises never intended for anyone else to read. He may have left sentences unfinished, abbreviated references that only he needed to understand, or shifted thought mid-sentence without bothering to clean up what came before. We cannot always distinguish between a corruption introduced by a scribe in the ninth century, a misprint by Gessner's printing workshop in 1558/59, and a fragment that Marcus himself simply never finished writing. The honest answer, in many cases, is that we do not know, and this translation does not pretend otherwise.

Where the Xylander text is clearly corrupted, I have turned to modern critical editions and noted the discrepancy in the footnotes. The reader can see, in every significant case, exactly where the sources diverge and which reading was adopted.

But where the Xylander Greek and the modern critical editions simply disagree, where both readings are defensible and the choice between them is a matter of editorial judgment rather than obvious correction, I have generally preferred the Xylander reading, but there are cases where the Xylander text is clearly incorrect. This is a deliberate methodological choice. The principle of *lectio difficilior potior*, that the more difficult or unusual reading is more likely to be original because scribes tend to simplify rather than complicate, supports this approach in many cases. A later editor who found a passage awkward, blunt, or philosophically unusual would be more likely to emend it than to introduce the difficulty. The Xylander text, being earlier in the editorial chain, preserves more of these difficult readings.

The result is a translation that sits in a different place than any other currently available English version of *Meditations*. It is not a translation of the modern critical Greek, filtered through centuries of scholarly consensus. It is a translation grounded in the earliest printed text available, corrected and noted where that text is broken, but otherwise allowed to stand on its own terms. It is, as far as I am aware, a fresh approach. Every other English translation I have encountered takes the modern critical editions as its starting point and works forward. This translation starts with Xylander and works outward, using the modern editions as a check rather than a foundation.

There is one more consequence of this approach that the reader will notice, and I want to address it directly: this translation will not always read like polished English prose. The reader would be correct in that observation. It is deliberate.

Marcus did not write polished prose. He wrote in fragments, compressed phrases, abrupt pivots of thought, and the kind of shorthand that a person uses when writing only for himself. Koine Greek grammar is already alien to English word order, and Marcus's private notebook style compresses it further. Most translators resolve this by rewriting his sentences into fluent English, rearranging clauses, supplying transitions, and smoothing out the rhythm until Marcus sounds like an essayist composing for publication. The result reads well. It also reads like someone other than Marcus Aurelius, a Roman emperor, a Stoic philosopher, and a person deeply educated in Graeco-Roman literature, theology, and metaphysics.

I have chosen, wherever possible, to retain the Greek rendering as Marcus wrote it. Where he is abrupt, the English is abrupt. Where his thought arrives in fragments, the fragments are preserved. Where his grammar would strike an English reader as unusual, I have kept it unusual rather than normalizing it into something more comfortable. The goal is not elegant English. The goal is the closest possible approximation of what Marcus actually put on the page, and how he put it there.

In practice, this meant taking what were often fragmentary Koine Greek phrases and stitching them into readable English sentences, often joined by commas, semicolons, colons, or split into shorter sentences where the Greek phrasing naturally breaks. I have not left the text as raw, unparsed fragments; the result is meant to be readable, but readable is not the same as smooth. I have consistently chosen fidelity to Marcus's voice over fluency. If a sentence feels like it was written by a man thinking his way through a problem in real time rather than crafting a finished argument, that is because it was, and this translation tries to preserve that quality rather than edit it away. There are sentences that stretch on for entire paragraphs, pasted together with commas, colons, and semicolons. It is that way because that was how Marcus wrote it.

Whether that approach produces a better translation is for the reader to judge. What I can say is that it produces a different one, and in places, a noticeably different one. The footnotes document every significant divergence, so the reader is never left guessing which source is behind any given passage. The Xylander text has its limitations. The modern critical editions have their biases. This translation attempts to navigate between the two, using each to illuminate the other, and letting the reader see the seams.

A Note on the Order of the Books

Modern editions of *Meditations* present Book 1 as the beginning. This is how the text has been read for centuries, and it is the order in which the books are numbered. But there is reason to question whether Book 1 was actually the first book Marcus wrote, or whether it was, in fact, the last.

The evidence begins with the Xylander texts. In both the Greek and Latin editions of 1558/59, the heading "AMONG THE QUADI, BY THE GRANUA" appears within Book 1, not as a header to Book 2. Furthermore, what modern editors number as sections 2.1, 2.2, and 2.3 also appear within Book 1 in the Xylander text. It was the 17th-century editor Thomas Gataker[2] who moved these sections to the beginning of Book 2, where they have remained in every major edition since. This translation follows the modern convention in placing 2.1 through 2.3 in Book 2, but preserves the "AMONG

THE QUADI, BY THE GRANUA" heading at the end of Book 1, where it appears in the *editio princeps*.

The Granua (modern Hron River, Slovakia) flows through the territory of the Quadi, where Marcus was actively campaigning in 179-180 CE. Marcus died in March of 180 at Vindobona (modern Vienna), roughly 150 kilometers away, never leaving this theater of war. This places the composition of at least the final portion of Book 1 in the last months of Marcus's life.

The content supports this reading. Book 1 is not a philosophical meditation in the manner of the other eleven books. It is something quite different: a systematic accounting of debts. Marcus works through every significant person in his life, from his grandfather to the Gods themselves, recording what he received from each. It reads less like the beginning of a philosophical notebook and more like the summing-up of a life. The tone is retrospective, grateful, and final. It is, in essence, a farewell.

Consider also the sections that the Xylander text originally placed after the Quadi heading, within Book 1. In what is now numbered 2.2, Marcus tells himself: "You are an old man. Do not let it be enslaved any longer." He speaks of the flesh as "gore, and small bones, and a little woven network of nerves, veins, and arteries." In 2.3, he turns to Providence, Necessity, and the Changes of the Elements. These are the reflections of a man confronting his own mortality in a way that is immediate and personal, not abstract. Read as a continuation of Book 1, they transform the gratitude list into something more: a man who has accounted for his debts now turns to face his own dissolution.

It is my hypothesis that "Book 1" was not the first book Marcus wrote but the last. The numbered ordering of the books may reflect the order in which they were found or arranged by later editors, not the order of composition. A man on his final campaign, knowing he is old and ill, writing by the Granua in the winter of 179-180 CE, would have had every reason to end with an accounting of his debts to the people who shaped him.

This is speculation, not established fact. The manuscript tradition does not preserve dates of composition for the individual books, and scholars have debated the ordering for centuries. A. S. L. Farquharson, in his 1944 commentary, noted that the Quadi and Carnuntum headings are "now generally thought to be titles to Book 2 and Book 3" rather than colophons to the preceding books, and he observed that Books 2, 3, and 12 are "remarkably alike in matter and manner," suggesting they may have been composed close together in time. But the question of whether Book 1 was composed first or last remains open.

If Book 1 is indeed the last thing Marcus wrote, then the *Meditations* does not begin with gratitude. It ends with it. And the final image is not a philosopher beginning his work, but an emperor finishing his, by a frozen river at the edge of his empire, in the last winter of his life.

The Xylander Introductions

I have included the original introductory texts from the Xylander edition at the end of this book, after the twelve books of *Meditations* proper. I placed them there deliberately: this is a translation of Marcus Aurelius, and I did not want prefatory material from 16th-century editors to become the focus or to stand between the reader and the text. They are included for completeness, not prominence.

Four texts are included:

Xylander's Dedicatory Epistle is the letter Wilhelm Xylander wrote to his patron Georg von Stetten the Younger upon publishing the 1558/59 Latin edition. It is part dedication, part scholarly confession. Xylander praises Marcus as both philosopher and emperor, sketches his character from ancient sources, and then turns remarkably candid about the difficulties of his task: the damaged manuscript, the grueling translation, the places where he had to guess. He defends publishing an imperfect work rather than letting it remain unknown, and his honesty about the limitations of his own edition is itself a valuable piece of the textual history.

The Suda Lexicon excerpts are brief ancient biographical entries about Marcus Aurelius that Xylander included as prefatory context. They contain anecdotes about Marcus's devotion to philosophy even in old age, his character as described by ancient historians, and a summary of his reign.

These are drawn from the *Suda*, a 10th-century Byzantine encyclopedia that preserved fragments of earlier historical sources.

The Epitome of Sextus Aurelius Victor is a brief historical account of Marcus's reign drawn from a late Roman biographical compendium. It covers the relentless crises of his rule: wars across the East, Illyricum, Italy, and Gaul; earthquakes, plagues, floods, and locusts. It describes his character, his famous auction of imperial furnishings to fund the army without taxing the provinces, the revolt of Cassius, and his death at Vindobona. It ends with the Senate assembling in mourning and the Roman people presuming, as they had with Romulus, that Marcus had been received into heaven. As a historical source it is concise, but it captures the scale of what Marcus endured and the esteem in which he was held.

Conrad Gessner's Greek Dedicatory Epistle is the letter that accompanied the Greek text, addressed to Anton Werther von Bechlingen. Gessner frames *Meditations* within a Christian theological context, comparing Stoic virtue to Christian teaching and arguing that pagan philosophy, while incomplete, serves as a kind of preparation for Christian wisdom. His epistle is a fascinating artifact of 16th-century intellectual life: a devout Christian scholar explaining why a pagan emperor's private notebooks deserve publication. It also provides crucial details about the provenance of the Greek manuscript, tracing it through the library of Prince Otto Henry of the Palatinate.

Together, the dedicatory epistles by Xylander and Gessner document the circumstances under which *Meditations* first entered the printed world. They are the voices of the men who saved this work from obscurity, and they deserve to be heard, even if from the back of the book.

The Xylander edition also contained a Greek text and Latin translation of Marinus of Neapolis's *De Procli Vita et Foelicitate Liber* (*On the Life of Proclus and His Happiness*), a biography of the Neoplatonist philosopher Proclus, published there for the first time. It was a separate work bound alongside *Meditations* in the same volume. I have chosen not to include it here, as the focus of this book is Marcus Aurelius's *Meditations* alone.

1

Book 1

MARCUS ANTONINUS EMPEROR: To Himself. Book 1.

1.1 From my grandfather Verus:[3] good character and freedom from anger.

1.2 From the reputation and memory of my father:[4] modesty and a manly character.

1.3 From my mother:[5] Reverence for the Gods and generosity; and restraint not only from doing evil, but from even entertaining such a thought; further, simplicity in way of living, and a life far removed from the ways of the rich.

1.4 From my great-grandfather:[6] not to have frequented public schools, and to have employed good teachers at home, and to have learned that on such things one should spend generously.

1.5 From my tutor:[7] not to become a partisan of the Green or Blue chariot factions[8], nor of the Parmularius or Scutarius gladiators[9]; to endure labor and to need little; to work with my own hands and not meddle in the affairs of others; and to be unreceptive to slander.

1.6 From Diognetus:[10] freedom from empty pursuits; and to distrust what is said by miracle-workers and charlatans about incantations and the casting out of Daimons and such things; not to rear quails,[11] nor to be excited about such things.

To tolerate frank speech and to become familiar with Philosophy; to have heard Baccheius first, then Tandasis and Marcianus;[12] to have written dialogues as a boy; and to have desired a camp bed and animal skin, and whatever else belongs to the Greek training.[13]

1.7 From Rusticus:[14] to have received the Impression that my character needed correction and healing; not to have been diverted into sophistic zeal, nor to write on theoretical matters, nor to deliver exhortatory little speeches, nor to make a showy display of myself as an ascetic or as a benefactor;[15] and to have abstained from rhetoric, poetry, and refined speech.

Not to walk about at home in a robe, nor to do other such things; to write letters in a plain style, like the one he himself wrote to my mother from Sinuessa.[16]

To be disposed toward those who have been offended and transgressed to be easily called back and easy to converse with,[17] as soon as they themselves are willing to return; to read carefully and not be satisfied with a superficial overview; not to give hasty Assent to those who chatter; and to have encountered the memoirs of Epictetus,[18] which he shared with me from his own collection.

1.8 From Apollonius:[19] freedom, and an unhesitating refusal to leave anything to chance; to look to nothing else, even for a moment, except Reason; and to remain always the same, even in sharp pains, in the loss of a child, and in long illness.

To have seen clearly, in a living example, that the same man can be both most intense and most relaxed; not to be irritable when explaining things; to have seen a man who clearly regarded his experience and skill in transmitting doctrines as the least of his merits; and to have learned how to receive apparent favors from friends, neither becoming servile because of them nor receiving them ungraciously.

1.9 From Sextus:[20] Benevolence; an example of a household governed in a fatherly way; the concept of living according to Nature; to be dignified without pretense; attentiveness to the needs of friends with caring concern; tolerance of the unlearned; and to be unobtrusive toward those who merely hold opinions.

To be adaptable toward all people, so that his company was more pleasant than any flattery, and yet he was most respected by those very people at that very moment; and his ability to discover and organize, with sure comprehension and in methodical order, the Principles necessary for life.

Never to have shown any sign of Anger or any other Passion, but to be at the same time utterly free from Passion and yet full of Natural Affection; to speak well of others unobtrusively; and to possess deep learning without showing it off.

1.10 From Alexander the Grammarian:[21] Not to be censorious. Nor to criticize insultingly those who utter a barbarism, or a solecism, or something grating; but skillfully to pronounce the very word that ought to have been spoken, by way of a sufficient answer,[22] or confirmation, or joint inquiry about the thing itself rather than the word, or by some other such tactful reminder.[23]

1.11 From Fronto:[24] to have observed what tyrannical envy, craftiness, and hypocrisy are like; and that, generally speaking, those among us whom we call "well-born" are somehow rather lacking in Natural Affection.

1.12 From Alexander the Platonist:[25] Not to say to anyone often and without necessity, nor to write in a letter: "I am busy"; nor in this manner to constantly evade the Appropriate Actions pertaining to our relationships with those who share our life, citing surrounding affairs as an excuse.

1.13 From Catulus:[26] not to neglect a friend's complaint, even if he happens to be complaining irrationally, but to try to restore things to the accustomed footing; to speak enthusiastically in praise of one's teachers, as in the stories told about Domitius and Athenodotus;[27] and to have a genuine love for one's children.

1.14 From my brother Severus:[28] love of family, love of Truth, and love of Justice; through him, to have come to know Thrasea, Helvidius, Cato, Dion, Brutus;[29] and to have formed the Impression of a state governed by equal laws, administered with equal rights and equal freedom of speech; and of a monarchy that honors above all else the freedom of the governed.

From him, too, consistent and unwavering honor for Philosophy; to be beneficent, lavishly generous, and full of good hope; trust that he was loved by his friends; frankness toward those who incurred his censure; and that his friends had no need to guess what he wanted or did not want, for it was clear.

1.15 From Maximus:[30] to master yourself and not to be carried away by anything; to be cheerful in all circumstances, including illness; a well-balanced character, at once gentle and dignified; and to accomplish the task set before you without strain.

That everyone trusted him, that what he said, he meant, and that what he did, he did without malice; to be neither astonished nor startled; nowhere hurried, nor hesitating, nor at a loss, nor dejected, nor wearing a forced smile; nor again angry or suspicious.

To do good deeds, be forgiving, and to be truthful; and to give the impression of one who could not be straightened further, because he was never bent in the first place; and that no one ever thought himself looked down upon by him, nor would he have tolerated anyone presuming himself superior to him; and to make gracious jokes.

1.16 From my Father:[31] a gentle disposition, and unshakable adherence to decisions made after full examination; freedom from vanity regarding so-called honors; love of work and perseverance; to be ready to listen to those who have anything to contribute to the public good; to give to each according to merit, impartially; and to know from experience when to be strict and when to be lenient.

To have put a stop to the erotic Passions for boys.[32]

His public-spiritedness: he released his friends from the obligation always to dine with him or strictly accompany him on his travels; and those who were left behind for necessary reasons always found him the same man when he returned.

In councils: precise scrutiny and persistence, never withdrawing prematurely from inquiry, nor satisfied with first Impressions.

The preservation of friendships: never growing weary of them, nor being excessively fond. Self-sufficiency in all things, and a cheerful face. To foresee things from afar, and to arrange the smallest details without dramatic display.

The checking of acclamations and all flattery.

The ever-watchful guarding of the things necessary to the Empire, the economical management of its resources, and the endurance of the blame that comes from such frugality.

Regarding the Gods, not superstitious; and regarding men, not a demagogue, nor obsequious, nor a mob-pleaser, but sober in all things, and firm, never lacking in taste, nor a chaser of novelties.

And regarding the things that make life comfortable (of which Fortune provided in abundance), to use them without pretension and without apology; so as to enjoy them naturally when present, but not to need them when absent.

And that no one could say he was a sophist, a home-bred buffoon,[33] or a pedant; but a ripe man, a complete man, above flattery, capable of presiding over his own affairs and those of others.

In addition to these things, he honored those who genuinely practiced Philosophy, and to the others he was not insulting, nor was he led astray by them.[34] He was sociable, and gracious without being sickening.

And the care of his own body in due measure, not as one who clings to life, nor for the sake of adornment, nor yet neglectfully; but just enough that, through his own attentiveness, he very rarely needed a physician, or drugs, or poultices.

And above all, yielding without envy to those who possessed some particular faculty, such as eloquence, or knowledge of laws, or customs, or other matters, and supporting them so that each might be honored according to his own unique gifts. And acting always according to the ancestral ways, yet not trying to make a display of preserving the ancestral ways.

And not being prone to restless shifting, but staying in the same places and the same routines. And after sharp headaches, returning immediately fresh and vigorous to his usual activities. And not having many secrets, but very few and rare, and only concerning public matters.

And prudence and moderation in the giving of spectacles, the construction of public works, distributions, and such things, as a man who looked to what needed to be done, not to the reputation gained from doing it.

He did not bathe at odd hours;[35] he did not have a passion for building structures; he was not particular about foods, nor the textures and colors of fabrics, nor the beauty of slaves.[36]

The clothing from Lorium going up from the lower villa, and many of the things at Lanuvium; to the tax collector[37] in Tusculum,[38] whom he made an excuse about how he used it; and all such manner of behavior.[39]

There was nothing harsh, nor relentless, nor violent, nor, as one might say, "carried to the sweating point"; but all things were reasoned out individually, as at leisure, calmly, methodically, vigorously, consistently.

And one might apply to him what is recorded of Socrates: that he was able both to abstain from and to enjoy those things which many are too weak to abstain from and too indulgent in enjoying. But to be strong and enduring in both, and to be sober, is the mark of a man who possesses a perfect and invincible Psyche, just as this was shown in the illness of Maximus.[40]

1.17 From the Gods: To have good grandfathers, good parents, a good sister, good teachers, good intimates, good kinsmen, and friends, almost all of them. And that I did not fall into offending any of them; although I had such a disposition that, had the occasion arisen, I might well have done something of the sort; but the beneficence of the Gods ensured that no confluence of circumstances arose which would have been likely to expose me.

That I was not raised any longer with the concubine of my grandfather.

That I preserved the bloom of my youth, that I did not become a man before the proper time, but even gained additional time.

That I was placed under a ruler and a father who was destined to strip away all my vanity, and to bring me to the understanding that it is possible to live in a palace without needing bodyguards, conspicuous clothes, torches and statues, and other such pomp; but that one may draw oneself very close to the station of a private citizen, and yet, by Zeus, without becoming more servile or more lax in matters that must be handled with authority for the common interest.

To have had such a brother who, through his character, awakened me to take care of myself, and at the same time delighted me with honor and Natural Affection; that my children were neither dull-witted nor deformed in body.

That I did not advance further in rhetoric, poetry, and the other pursuits in which I might have been absorbed, had I felt myself making good progress; to have been quick to place my tutors in the positions of honor they seemed to desire, and not to have put them off with the hope that I would do it later, since they were still young.

To have known Apollonius, Rusticus, Maximus.

And to have received clear and frequent Impressions of the life according to Nature: what sort of thing it is; so that, as far as it depends on the Gods, and their communications, assistance, and inspirations, nothing prevents me already from living according to Nature. But that I still fall short of this through my own fault, and through not observing the reminders and what are virtually the teachings of the Gods.

That my body has held out so long in such a kind of life.

To have touched neither Benedicta nor Theodotus.[41] And that later, even when I did fall into erotic Passions, I was cured.

That, though I was often angry with Rusticus, I never went any further, to do anything for which I would have felt regret.

That, though my mother was fated to die young, she nevertheless spent her final years with me.

That whenever I wished to help someone in poverty or some other need, I never had to hear that "there is no money from which it might come." And that I myself never fell into a similar need, such that I would have had to receive from another.

That my wife is such as she is: so obedient, so affectionate, and so simple.[42]

That I had an abundance of suitable caretakers for my children.

That through dreams, remedies were given to me, among other things, especially against spitting blood and against dizziness; and this at Caieta,[43] as if by an oracle.[44]

And how, when I desired Philosophy, I did not fall into the hands of a sophist, nor sit down to write treatises, or to analyze syllogisms, or to busy myself with celestial speculations. For all these things require the help of the Gods and Fortune.

AMONG THE QUADI, BY THE GRANUA[45]

2

Book 2

2.1 At dawn, forewarn yourself: I shall encounter the meddlesome, the ungrateful, the insolent, the deceitful, the spiteful, and the unsociable. All this has befallen them because of their ignorance of Good and Evil. But I, having contemplated the Nature of the Good (that it is noble) and of the Evil (that it is shameful) and the Nature of the very one who errs (that he is my kinsman, not by the same blood or seed, but as a partaker of Intellect and a Divine Portion), I cannot be harmed by any of them; for no one will impose on me with what is shameful. Nor can I be angry with my kinsman, or hate him. For we were born for cooperation, like feet, like hands, like eyelids, like the rows of upper and lower teeth. Therefore, to work against one another is contrary to Nature; and to be indignant and to turn away is to work against one another.

2.2 Whatever this is that I am, it is a little flesh, a little Pneuma, and the Ruling Faculty. Put aside your books; be distracted no longer; it is not permitted. But, as if you were already dying, despise the flesh: it is gore, and small bones, and a little woven network of nerves, veins, and arteries. And look at the Pneuma: what sort of thing it is: wind, and not even always the same, but every hour vomited out and gulped back in. The third, then, is the Ruling

Faculty. Consider this: you are an old man. Do not let it[46] be enslaved any longer. Do not let it be pulled about like a puppet any longer by unsociable Impulse. Do not resent what is fated in the present, nor dread what is to come.

2.3 The things of the Gods are full of Providence. The things of Fortune are not without Nature, or without the spinning-together and intertwining of things governed by Providence. All things flow from there. Moreover, there is Necessity, and that which benefits the whole Cosmos, of which you are a part. For every part of Nature, that is good which the Nature of the Whole brings forth, and which serves to preserve it. The Cosmos is preserved by the Transformations of the Elements, and likewise by the Changes of the Compounds. Let these things be enough for you, and let them always be your Doctrines. But cast away your thirst for books, so that you may not die grumbling, but truly cheerful, and with heartfelt gratitude to the Gods.

2.4 Remember how long you have been putting off these things, and how many appointed terms you have received from the Gods and yet do not use. You must now at last perceive of what Cosmos you are a part, and of what Governor of the Cosmos you have come into being as an emanation; and that a limit of time is fixed for you, which, if you do not use it to clear the sky, will be gone, and you will be gone, and the chance will not come again.

2.5 Every hour, attend firmly, as a Roman and a man, to what is in your hands: to act with precise and unfeigned dignity, Natural Affection, freedom, and Justice; and to grant yourself leisure from all other Impressions. And you will achieve this if you perform every act of your life as though it were your last: freed from all aimlessness, all passionate aversion from the guidance of Reason, all hypocrisy, self-love, and dissatisfaction with what has been allotted to you. Do you see how few things there are which, if a man masters them, he is able to live a well-flowing, God-like[47] life? For even the Gods will demand nothing more from one who guards these things.

2.6 Dishonor, dishonor yourself, O Psyche! You will no longer have the opportunity to honor yourself; for each has but one life, and yours is nearly finished; yet you are not revering yourself, but placing your well-being in the Psyches of others.

2.7 Do the things falling upon you from outside distract you?

Give yourself leisure to learn something good besides, and stop drifting. But now you must also guard against the other distraction: for those who are wearied by life talk nonsense even through their actions, having no aim toward which they direct every Impulse and indeed every Impression.

2.8 No one has easily been seen to be miserable on account of not attending to what goes on in another's Psyche; but those who do not follow closely the movements of their own Psyche are necessarily miserable.

2.9 One must always remember these things: what the Nature of the Whole is, and what mine is, and how the latter stands in relation to the former (what kind of part, of what kind of Whole) and that no one prevents you from always doing and saying the things consequent upon the Nature of which you are a part.

2.10 In his comparison of faults, Theophrastus[48] speaks philosophically, as one might compare such things in a rather general way, when he says that the transgressions committed through Desire are more grievous than those committed through anger. For the angry man seems to turn away from Reason with pain and a kind of unconscious contraction; but he who errs through Desire, being overcome by Pleasure, seems in a way more undisciplined and more womanish in his offenses.

Rightly, then, and in a way worthy of Philosophy, he said that the offense committed with Pleasure is subject to greater blame than that committed with pain. On the whole, the one is more like a man who has been wronged first and, through pain, is compelled to anger; but the other has set out of his own accord toward wrongdoing, being carried toward action by Desire.

2.11 As if it is possible to depart from life at any moment, act, [speak][49], and think accordingly. To depart from among men, if there are Gods, is nothing terrible; for they would not involve you in harm. But if either they do not exist or they have no concern for human affairs, why should I live in a Cosmos empty of Gods or empty of Providence?

But they do exist, and they do care about human things. And as for things truly evil, so that man might not fall into them, they have placed the whole matter in his power. And as for the remaining things, if any of them were evil, they would have foreseen even this, so that it would be entirely in every man's power not to fall into it.

But that which does not make a man worse, how can it make a man's life worse?

The Nature of the Whole would not have overlooked such things either through ignorance, or through knowing yet being unable to guard against or correct them; nor would it have committed so great an error, whether through lack of power or lack of skill, as to let good things and evil things fall equally and indiscriminately upon both good men and evil men.

Death, I say, and Life, Glory and Disgrace, Pain and Pleasure, Wealth and Poverty; all these things befall good and evil men equally, being neither noble nor shameful; therefore they are neither Good nor Evil.

2.12 How quickly all things vanish: in the Cosmos, the bodies themselves; in Eternity, the memories of them. Of what sort are all perceptible things, and especially those that entice with Pleasure, or terrify with pain, or are trumpeted abroad by vanity! How cheap and contemptible, filthy, easily corruptible, and dead! It is for the Intellectual Power to consider these things.

What sort of people are those whose opinions and voices confer good reputation? What is it to die?

If one looks at it in itself alone, and by analysis of the concept strips away the imaginings projected upon it, one will conceive of it as nothing other than a function of Nature. If anyone fears a function of Nature, he is a child. This indeed is not only a function of Nature, but also something beneficial to her. Consider how man touches God, and through what part of himself, and when that part of man is so disposed.

2.13 Nothing is more wretched than a man who goes around in circles, and, as the saying goes, "searches beneath the earth,"[50] seeking by conjecture what is in the Psyches of his neighbors, yet not perceiving that it suffices to attend to the Daimon[51] within him alone, and to tend it genuinely. And the tending of it consists in keeping it pure from Passion, heedlessness, and dissatisfaction with what comes from Gods and men. For the things from the Gods are worthy of reverence on account of their Virtue; and the things from men are dear on account of kinship; though sometimes, in a way, they are even pitiable, on account of ignorance of Good and Evil. This disability is no less a crippling than that which deprives one of the ability to distinguish white from black.

2.14 Even if you were going to live three thousand years, or as many myriads, still remember that no one loses any other life than the one he is living, nor does he live any other life than the one he loses. The longest, therefore, comes to the same as the shortest. For the Present is equal for all, and what is perishing is therefore equal, and thus what is being lost is revealed to be momentary. For no one could lose either the Past or the Future; for how could anyone take from him what he does not possess?

One must remember, then, these two things: first, that all things from Eternity are of the same kind and recur in cycles, and it makes no difference whether one will see the same things in a hundred years, or two hundred, or in infinite time; second, that the longest-lived and the one who will die soonest lose the same: for the Present alone is that of which one is to be deprived (if indeed one possesses even this alone) and what one does not possess, one cannot lose.

2.15 Everything is Opinion. For clear indeed are the things said by Monimos the Cynic;[52] and clear also is the usefulness of what was said, if one accepts what is palatable in it only as far as it is true.

2.16 The Psyche of man does violence to itself: most of all when it becomes, so far as lies in its power, an abscess and, as it were, a tumor on the Cosmos. For to be indignant at anything that happens is a revolt from Nature, in which the natures of all other things are contained as parts.

Next, when it turns away from any man, or even moves against him so as to do harm, as the Psyches of the angry do.

Third, when it is overcome by Pleasure or Pain.

Fourth, when it plays a part, and does or says anything with pretense and untruthfully.

Fifth, when it directs any action and Impulse of its own toward no target, but performs anything whatsoever randomly and without attention; when it is necessary that even the smallest things be done with reference to the Goal. And the Goal of Rational Animals is to follow the Reason and law of the most ancient city and Commonwealth.[53]

2.17 Of human life: its time is a point; its Substance, flowing; its perception, dim; the Composition of the whole Body, easily rotted; the Psyche, a spinning top; Fortune, hard to conjecture; fame, without judgment. To sum up: all the things of the Body are a river; the things of the Psyche, a dream and vapor; life is a war and a stranger's sojourn; and posthumous fame is oblivion.

What, then, is able to guide a man through?

One thing alone: Philosophy. And this consists in guarding the Daimon within free from outrage and unharmed, superior to Pleasures and Pains, doing nothing randomly, nothing with falsehood or pretense; feeling no need for another to do or not do anything; and furthermore, accepting what happens and what is allotted as coming from the same source from which he himself came; and above all, awaiting death with a gracious mind, seeing it as nothing other than the Dissolution of the Elements from which each living thing is composed. For if to the Elements themselves there is nothing terrible in each continually transforming into another, why should one look with apprehension upon the Transformation and Dissolution of all things? For it is according to Nature; and nothing is Evil which is according to Nature.

3

Book 3

MARCUS ANTONINUS EMPEROR: To Himself. Book 3.

These writings in Carnuntum.[54]

3.1 We must consider not only that life is used up each day and a smaller part remains, but also this: that even if someone should live longer, it is unclear whether the Mind will still suffice for comprehending things and for the contemplation that contributes to understanding both Divine and human matters. For if one begins to rave, the breathing, nourishment, forming of Impressions, Impulses, and everything else of that sort will not fail. But the power to make use of oneself, to accurately reckon the considerations of Approproate Action, to analyze what presents itself, to reflect upon whether it is already time for oneself to depart, and all such things as require thoroughly exercised reasoning: these are extinguished first. One must therefore make haste, not only because one draws ever nearer to death, but also because the comprehension of things and the capacity to follow them attentively ceases beforehand.

3.2 One must also observe things like this: that even the byproducts of what happens according to Nature possess a certain grace and allure. For

15

instance, when bread is baked, some parts crack open. These splits, though in a way contrary to the baker's art and not conforming to its intention, are somehow attractive and arouse an eagerness for the food in their own way. Likewise, figs at their ripest gape open, and in tree-ripened olives, the very nearness to decay lends the fruit a distinctive beauty. Likewise, the drooping ears of grain, the lion's scowl, the foam streaming from boars' mouths, and many other things, though far from beautiful when examined in isolation, nonetheless lend adornment and captivate the Psyche because they accompany what happens according to Nature.

Thus, if anyone has deep feeling and insight into what comes to be in the Whole, almost nothing, not even among the things that occur as consequences, will fail to seem pleasingly composed in its own way. And he will look upon the real gaping jaws of wild beasts with no less pleasure than upon the imitations that painters and sculptors display. And he will be able to see, with his own temperate eyes, a certain prime and beauty even in an old woman and an old man, and the charm in children. And many such things will present themselves, things whose appeal is not evident to everyone, but only to one genuinely familiar with Nature and her works.

3.3 Hippocrates,[55] after curing many diseases, himself fell ill and died. The Chaldeans,[56] after predicting the deaths of many, were themselves overtaken by Fate. Alexander, Pompey, and Gaius Caesar,[57] having so many times utterly destroyed whole cities and cut down tens of thousands of cavalry and infantry in battle, at last departed from life themselves. Heraclitus,[58] after his many inquiries into the Conflagration of the Cosmos, died swollen with water and smeared with cowshit. Lice destroyed Democritus, and other lice destroyed Socrates.[59]

What do these things mean?

You have embarked, you have made your voyage, you have arrived: disembark. If to another life, the Gods are there also; but if to a state without sensation, you will cease to be subject to Pains and Pleasures, and will cease being enslaved to a vessel so much baser[60] than what it serves. For the one is Intellect and Daimon; the other is earth and gore.

3.4 Do not waste what remains of your life on Impressions about other people, unless your thinking genuinely serves the Common Good. When you do that, you rob yourself of other work. Instead, you fill your mind with questions like: "What is that person doing? Why? What is he saying? What is he planning?", all the chatter that pulls you away from watching over your own Ruling Faculty.

You must avoid, in the chain of your Impressions, anything random or idle, above all what is meddlesome and malignant, and train yourself to entertain only those thoughts which, if someone suddenly asked "What are you thinking right now?" you could answer immediately with complete frankness.

From that answer it should be immediately clear that everything in you is straightforward and kindly, worthy of a Social Animal, someone who disregards Impressions seeking Pleasure as an end, along with any thought of rivalry, envy, or suspicion, and anything else you would be ashamed to confess having in your mind. The man who has stopped postponing his place among the best becomes a priest and servant of the Gods, making use of the Daimon established within him.

That Daimon keeps him unstained by Pleasure, unharmed by Pain, untouched by any insult, and unaffected by all baseness. He is an athlete in the greatest contest: that of not being overthrown by any Passion. He is dyed through with Justice and embraces with his whole Psyche whatever happens and all that is allotted to him. Such a man only rarely (and never without genuine necessity for the Common Good) allows his mind to dwell on what another person is saying, doing, or thinking.

His concern is with what is his own: the work he was born for. He keeps his attention on what portion of reality the Whole is spinning out for him and makes his own actions beautiful, trusting that his lot is good. He also keeps in mind that every Rational being is his kinsman, and that to care for all human beings is in accord with Human Nature. But he does not treat everyone's approval as worth pursuing: only that of those who clearly live in agreement with Nature. As for the others, he remembers clearly what kind of people they are, in public and in private, by night and by day, and the company in which they wallow. Therefore he does not value praise from those who cannot even satisfy themselves.

3.5 Neither act unwillingly, nor unsocially, nor without examination, nor with inner conflict. Do not let over-subtlety beautify your Mind; neither be a man of many words nor someone who meddles in too many things. Further, let the God within you be the guardian of a male animal, an elder, a statesman, a Roman, a ruler, one who has stationed himself at his post like someone awaiting the recall signal from life, ready for release, needing neither oath nor witness from any other person. And let there be cheerfulness, independence from external assistance, and no need for the peace that others provide. You must stand upright, not be propped up.

3.6 If you find in human life anything better than Justice, Truth, Temperance, and Courage, in short, anything better than your own Mind's contentment with itself in those matters where it enables you to act according to right Reason, and its contentment with Fate in those things allotted without your choice; if, I say, you see anything better than this, turn to it with your whole Psyche and enjoy the best thing you have found. But if nothing appears more excellent than the Daimon dwelling within you, which has subjected your own Impulses to itself, scrutinizes your Impressions, and has, as Socrates said, withdrawn itself from the persuasions of sense,[61] submitted itself to the Gods, and cares for mankind; if you find all other things to be trivial and worthless in comparison, then give no room to anything else.

For once you incline toward something else and are drawn away, you will no longer be able, without being torn asunder, to give undivided preference to that good which is properly your own. For it is wrong to set up any rival to the Rational and Civic Good,[62] not anything at all of a different kind: not the praise of the many, nor offices, nor wealth, nor the enjoyment of Pleasure. All these things, even if they seem to fit for a little while, may suddenly master you and lead you astray. But, I say, simply and freely choose what is best and hold to it.

"But what is best is what benefits me."

If it benefits you as a Rational being, then maintain it. But if as an animal only, then declare so and guard your judgment without arrogance, only ensure that your examination is sound.

3.7 Never value as advantageous to yourself anything that will compel you to break faith, abandon shame, hate anyone, suspect, curse, dissemble, or desire anything requiring walls and veils. For one who prioritizes his own Intellect and Daimon and the sacred rites of its Virtue plays no tragic part, utters no groans, and needs neither solitude nor crowd. Above all, he will live neither pursuing nor fleeing. Whether the Psyche will inhabit the body that envelops it for a longer or shorter time concerns him not at all. For even if he must depart immediately, he will go as readily as he would perform any other action that can be done with modesty and order. This one thing alone throughout life he guards: that the Mind not fall into any state alien to a Rational and Civic Animal.

3.8 In the Mind of the disciplined and purified person you will find nothing festering, nothing stained, nothing suppurating beneath the surface. Nor does Fate cut short an incomplete life, as one might say of a tragic actor who leaves the stage before finishing his role and completing the drama. Furthermore, you will find nothing servile, nothing affected, nothing dependent, nothing isolated, nothing accountable to another, nothing cowering.

3.9 Revere your capacity to form opinions. Everything depends on this: that your Ruling Faculty never entertains an Opinion contrary to Nature or to the Constitution of a Rational Animal. And this capacity ensures freedom from rashness, kinship with human beings, and following the Gods.

3.10 Therefore, cast all else aside and hold to these few things. And remember that each person lives only in this Present, this momentary thing. The rest is either past and gone, or is uncertain. Small indeed is the life that each person lives, and small the corner of the earth on which he lives it. Small, too, is even the longest-lasting posthumous fame, itself passed on through a succession of little men who will themselves soon die, and who do not even know themselves, much less the man long dead.

3.11 To the precepts I have mentioned, let this one be added: always make a definition or an outline of whatever Impression presents itself to your mind, so as to see what it is in its naked essence, both as a whole and in its parts. Tell yourself its proper name, and the names of those things of which it is composed and into which it will be resolved. Nothing is so conducive to Magnanimity as the ability to examine methodically and truthfully every object that we encounter in life, and always to look at things so as to grasp what use each serves in the Cosmos, what value it has for the Whole, and what value for the man who is a citizen of that Supreme City, of which other cities are but households.[63]

What is this thing? Of what is it composed, and for how long is it in its nature to endure, this thing that now makes an Impression on me?

And what Virtue is needed in its presence?

Gentleness, for instance; or Courage, truthfulness, faithfulness, simplicity, self-sufficiency, and the rest.

Therefore, in each case, one must say: this comes from God; this comes from the conjunction and intertwining of Fate, from coincidence and Fortune; this comes from my kinsman and my fellow citizen, who is ignorant of what is according to his Nature. But I am not ignorant, and so I treat him according to the natural law of Fellowship, with Benevolence and Justice. At the same time, in matters that are Indifferent, I strive to assess their proper value.

3.12 If you perform the task at hand, following right Reason, with diligence, vigor, and good will, and make nothing a side-issue, but keep the Daimon within you pure, as if you might have to give it back at any moment; if you hold to this, expecting nothing and avoiding nothing, but are content with your present action according to Nature and with heroic Truth in what you say and speak, you will live well. And there is no one who can prevent this.

3.13 Just as physicians always have their tools and surgical instruments at hand for sudden emergencies, so too should you have your Principles ready for the understanding of things Divine and human, and for the performance of every action, even the smallest, with remembrance of the link that unites the two. For you will not carry out any human duty well unless you refer it to the Divine, nor conversely.

3.14 Stop your roaming. For you will no longer read your own notebooks, nor the deeds of the ancient Romans and Greeks, nor the excerpts from writings which you were storing up for your old age.[64] Hasten, therefore, toward the end, and casting away empty hopes, help yourself, if you have any care for yourself, while you can.

3.15 They do not know how many things are signified by stealing, sowing, buying, keeping quiet, and seeing what must be done. This seeing is not done with the eyes, but with another kind of vision.

3.16 The Body has its Sensations. The Psyche has its Impulses. The Intellect has its Principles. To be imprinted by an Impression is common to us and to cattle. To be moved by the strings of Impulse is common to wild beasts, to effeminate men,[65] and to a Phalaris or a Nero.[66]

Yet to have the Intellect as guide toward what appears to be one's duty is common also to those who do not believe in the Gods,[67] to those who abandon their fatherland, and to those who do their shameful things once they have closed the doors. If, then, all other things are common to the beings I have mentioned, there remains what is proper to the good man: to welcome all that happens and is spun for him by Fate; not to muddy the Daimon that is enthroned in his breast, nor to disturb it with a throng of Impressions, but to keep it gracious, following God in an orderly way; speaking nothing contrary to the Truth and doing nothing contrary to Justice. And if all men refuse to believe that he lives a simple, modest, and cheerful life, he is not angry with any of them, nor does he swerve from the path that leads to the Goal of Life, to which he must come pure, calm, and ready to be released, in unforced harmony with his own Fate.

4

Book 4

MARCUS ANTONINUS EMPEROR: To Himself. Book 4.

4.1 The Ruling Faculty within, when it is in accordance with Nature, is so disposed toward what happens that it easily adapts itself to what is possible and what is presented. For it loves no designated Material, but sets its Impulse toward preferred things with Reservation; and whatever encounters it, whatever is brought against it, it makes into Material for itself. Just as a fire overpowers what falls into it, by which a small lamp would have been extinguished; but the blazing fire quickly appropriates what is cast upon it, and consumes it, and rises higher because of it.

4.2 Let no act be done at random, nor otherwise than according to a principle that completes the Art.

4.3 They seek retreats for themselves: country estates, and beaches, and mountains; and you too are accustomed to desiring such things most of all. But this is altogether the mark of the most common sort of person, when it is permitted to you, whenever you wish, to retreat into yourself. For nowhere does a man retreat to a more quiet or untroubled place than into his own Psyche, especially the man who has such things inside him that, by looking at them, he immediately becomes perfectly at ease. And by "ease" I mean nothing other than Good Order. Therefore, grant yourself this retreat continually and renew yourself. Let the principles be brief and elemental, ones which, as soon as you encounter them, will suffice to wash away the Distress and send you back without annoyance at those things to which you return.

For what are you annoyed with? The Vice of men?

Recall the judgment that Rational Animals were born for the sake of one another, and that tolerance is a part of Justice, and that they err unwillingly. And consider how many already, after feuding, suspecting, hating, and running one another through with spears, lie stretched out dead, reduced to ash. Desist at last.

But are you annoyed with what is assigned from the Whole?

Renew the disjunction: "Either Providence or Atoms";[68] or the arguments by which it was proven that the Cosmos is like a City.

Or do bodily things still have a hold on you?

Consider that the Mind, once it has reclaimed itself and recognized its own power, does not mingle with the smooth or rough movements of the Pneuma. And recall, furthermore, all that you have heard concerning Pain and Pleasure, to which you gave Assent.

Or will your petty ambition for fame distract you?

Look at the speed of the forgetfulness of all things, and the Chaos of boundless Eternity, before and after, the hollowness of the echo, the fickleness and lack of judgment in those who seem to praise, and the narrowness of the place in which it is circumscribed.

The whole earth is a point; and how small a corner of it is this place of habitation? And how many are here, and of what sort are they, who will praise you?

Therefore, remember the retreat into this little plot of land that is yourself. Above all, do not be wrenched about or overstrained, but be free, and look at things like a man, like a human being, like a citizen, like a mortal creature.

And among the principles most ready to hand, into which you will look, let there be these two:

First, that things do not touch the Psyche, but stand quiet outside it; disturbances come only from the internal Opinion.

Second, that all these things which you see will transform in a moment and will no longer exist; and constantly think on how many Changes you have already watched. The Cosmos is Alteration; Life is Opinion.

4.4 If the Intellectual faculty is common to us, then so is the Reason by which we are Rational; if this is true, then so too is the Reason which commands what to do and what not to do; if this is true, the Law too is common. If this is true, we are fellow citizens. If this is true, we share in a certain citizenship. If this is true, the Cosmos is like a City.

For of what other common citizenship can we say the whole human race partakes? And from there, from this common City, come the Intellectual, the Rational, and the Lawful capacities in us. Or where else could they come from?

Just as the earthy part of me has been portioned off from the Earth, the liquid from another element, the Pneumatic element from some source, and the hot and fiery from its own specific source (for nothing comes from nothing, just as nothing returns to non-being), so too does the Intellectual come from somewhere.

4.5 Death is like birth, a mystery of Nature: a Composition of the same Elements, and a Dissolution into them. On the whole, it is nothing one should be ashamed of, for it is not contrary to what befits an Intellectual Animal, nor to the Reason of its Constitution.[69]

4.6 Such things are naturally bound to come from people of that sort, of Necessity. He who wishes this not to be so, wishes for the fig tree to have no sap. But in general, remember this: within a very short time, both you and he will be dead. And soon after, not even your names will be left behind.

4.7 Remove the Judgment, and "I am harmed" is removed. Remove "I am harmed," and the harm is removed.

4.8 That which does not make a man worse than he was, does not make his life worse either, nor does it harm him, either from the outside or from the inside.

4.9 The Nature of what is Beneficial has been compelled to do this.

4.10 That everything that happens, happens justly; this you will find, if you watch closely. I do not mean merely in sequence, but in accordance with Justice, as though by one assigning what is due according to worth. Keep watch, then, as you have begun; and whatever you do, do it with this in mind: to be Good, in the specific sense in which "the Good man" is understood. Preserve this in every action.

4.11 Do not assume things as the man who outrages you judges them or as he wants you to judge them. Rather, see things as they are in Truth.

4.12 Two readinesses must always be at hand: first, to do only what the Kingly and Legislative Reason suggests for the benefit of humankind; second, to change your position if someone comes along to correct you and lead you away from some vain presumption. But this change must always proceed from some convincing ground of Justice or the Common Good, and the guiding considerations must be only of this kind, not because something appeared pleasant or glorious.

4.13 Have you Reason?
　I have.
　Why then do you not use it?
　For when this does its own work, what more do you want?

4.14 You came into being as a part. You will vanish into that which produced you; or rather, you will be received back into its Seminal Reason through Transformation.

4.15 Many grains of incense on the same altar: one falls sooner, another later, but it makes no difference.

4.16 Within ten days you will seem a God to those to whom you are now a wild beast and an ape, if you return to your Principles and to the worship of Reason.

4.17 Do not act as if you were going to live ten thousand years. Death hangs over you. While you live, while it is in your power, become good.

4.18 How much leisure he gains who does not look at what his neighbor said or did or thought, but only at what he himself does, so that this alone may be just and holy. As for the Good man: do not look around at black characters, but run straight on the line, not swerving.

4.19 He who is agitated about posthumous fame does not imagine that each one of those who remember him will himself also die very soon; and then again the one who succeeded him, until all memory is extinguished, as it passes through those being kindled and quenched.

But suppose those who will remember are immortal, and the memory immortal: what is that to you?

And I do not mean merely that it is nothing to the dead man, but to the living: what is praise?

Unless, perhaps, it serves some practical purpose. But set aside for now, as untimely, Nature's gift; that belongs to another line of reasoning.

4.20 Everything that is beautiful in any way is beautiful of itself, and complete in itself, not having praise as a part of it. The thing praised is made neither better nor worse. I say this also of things which are more commonly called beautiful, such as material things or works of art. For does the truly beautiful need anything?

No more than Law; no more than Truth; no more than Benevolence or Modesty.

Which of these is beautiful because it is praised, or destroyed if it is blamed?

Does an emerald become worse in itself if it is not praised? Or gold, or ivory, or purple, or a lyre,[70] or a blade, or a small blossom, or a sapling?

4.21 If Psyches remain, how does the air accommodate them from Eternity? How does the earth accommodate the bodies of those who have been buried for so much time?

Just as here the Transformation and Dissolution of these bodies, after a certain continued existence, makes room for other dead bodies; so too the Psyches transferred into the air, after remaining for a certain time, are transformed and diffused and kindled, being taken back into the Seminal Reason of the Whole; and in this way they make room for those who come to dwell there afterward. This is what one might answer on the assumption that Psyches do remain.

But one must not only consider the multitude of bodies being buried in this way, but also the multitude of animals being eaten each day by us and by the other animals.

For how great a number is consumed and thus, as it were, buried in the bodies of those who feed on them?

And yet space receives them through their conversion into blood, and through their alteration into the aerial or fiery element.

What is the investigation of Truth in this matter? A division into the Material and the Causal.

4.22 Do not wander off, but in every Impulse render what is Just, and in every Impression preserve the power of apprehension.

4.23 Everything harmonizes with me which harmonizes with you, O Cosmos. Nothing is too early or too late for me which is timely for you. Everything is fruit to me which your seasons bear. O Nature, from you are all things, in you are all things, into you are all things.

That man[71] says, "O beloved city of Cecrops";[72] will you not say, "O beloved city of Zeus"?

4.24 "Do few things," he says, "if you would be cheerful."

Is it not better to do what is necessary, and whatever the Reason of a creature Social by Nature selects, and in the manner it selects?

For this brings not only the cheerfulness that comes from doing well, but also that which comes from doing few things. For the greatest part of what we say and do is unnecessary; and if one strips this away, one will have more leisure and less disturbance.

On each occasion, therefore, one should remind oneself, "Is this not one of the unnecessary things?"

And one must remove not only unnecessary acts, but also unnecessary Impressions; for then superfluous acts will not follow.

4.25 Try how the life of the good person suits you too: the life of one who is content with what has been allotted from the Whole, and satisfied with his own just action and benevolent disposition.

4.26 Have you seen those things?

Look also at these. Do not disturb yourself. Make yourself simple.

Does a man do wrong?

He does wrong to himself.

Has something happened to you?

It is well. From the Whole, from the beginning, all that befalls you was co-fated with you and co-spun.

In sum, life is short. You must make the best of the present with sound Judgment and Justice. Be sober in your relaxation.

4.27 Either an ordered Cosmos, or a confused jumble; but surely a Cosmos.

Or can a kind of Cosmos subsist in you, while in the All there is Disorder? And this, when all things are thus separated, diffused, and bound in Sympathy?

4.28 The dark character: effeminate, obstinate, bestial, cattle-like, childish, stupid, fraudulent, buffoonish, hucksterish, tyrannical.

4.29 If he is a stranger to the Cosmos who does not know what exists in it, no less a stranger is he who does not know the things coming to be. An exile is he who flees from Civic Reason; blind is he who shuts the eye of his Intellect; a beggar is he who needs another and does not have within himself all things useful for life. An abscess on the Cosmos is he who withdraws and separates himself from the Reason of Common Nature by being dissatisfied with what happens, for that Nature bears this, the very one that also bore you. A torn-off piece of the City is he who separates his own Psyche from that of Rational beings, which is one.

4.30 One philosophizes without a tunic;[73] another without a book; another yet, half-naked.

"I have no bread," he says, "and I hold to Reason."

And I have no nourishment from my learning, and I hold fast.

4.31 Love the little art you learned, and find your rest in it. Go through the remainder of your life as one who has entrusted all your affairs to the Gods with your whole Psyche, making yourself neither a tyrant nor the slave of any human being.

4.32 Conceive, for the sake of argument, the times of Vespasian, and you will see all the same things: people marrying, raising children, falling sick, dying, waging war, keeping festivals, trading, farming, flattering, behaving arrogantly, suspecting, plotting, praying for some to die, grumbling about the present, loving, hoarding, desiring consulships and kingdoms. Well then, that life of theirs is no longer to be found anywhere.

Again, pass on to the times of Trajan. Again, all the same things. That life too is dead.[74]

Similarly, survey the records of other times and of whole nations, and see how many, after straining intensely, soon fell and were dissolved into the Elements. But above all, one must call to mind those whom you yourself have known straining after vanities, those who neglected to do what accords with their own natural Constitution, and to hold tenaciously to that, and to be content with it.

It is necessary here to remember that the Attention given to each action has its own proper worth and proportion. For thus you will not become irritably dissatisfied, so long as you do not busy yourself with lesser things beyond what is fitting.

4.33 The words which were once familiar are now archaisms. So too the names of those who were once much-sung are now, in a way, archaisms: Camillus, Caeso, Volesus, Leonnatus;[75] and a little after, Scipio and Cato; then Augustus, then Hadrian and Antoninus.[76] For all things fade and quickly become mythical; and quickly too complete oblivion buries them over. And these things I say of those who have blazed in some wondrous way; for the rest, as soon as they have breathed their last, they are "unknown and unheard of."

And what, after all, is everlasting remembrance?

Utter emptiness.

What, then, is it about which we must be earnest?

This one thing: a just Mind, Social Actions, Discourse such as never to prove false, and a Disposition embracing all that happens as necessary, as familiar, as flowing from such an origin and fount.

4.34 Willingly yield yourself to Clotho, allowing her to spin you along with whatever things she wishes.[77]

4.35 All things are ephemeral: both the rememberer and the remembered.

4.36 Observe constantly that all things take place by Transformation, and accustom yourself to think that the Nature of the Whole loves nothing so much as to transform existing things and to make new things like them. For all that exists is in a manner the seed of that which will be from it. But you imagine only those things cast into the earth or a womb to be seeds, and this is a very vulgar notion.

4.37 You will soon be dead, and you are not yet simple, nor free from disturbance, nor free from the suspicion of being harmed from outside, nor graciously disposed toward all, nor do you place Wisdom only in doing what is Just.

4.38 Look into their Ruling Faculties, even of the wise: what sorts of things they flee, and what sorts of things they pursue.

4.39 Your evil does not subsist in the Ruling Faculty of another, nor indeed in any variation or alteration of your bodily envelope. Where, then?

Where that which forms suppositions about evils resides: in you. Let this, then, form no such supposition, and all is well. And even if that which is nearest to it, your little body, is cut, burned, festers, or rots, yet let the part which forms suppositions about these things be quiet; that is, let it judge that nothing is either Bad or Good which can happen equally to a bad man and a good man. For that which happens equally to him who lives contrary to Nature and to him who lives according to Nature is neither according to Nature nor contrary to Nature.

4.40 Constantly conceive of the Cosmos as one living being, having one Substance and one Psyche: how all things are given over to one perception, its own; how it does all things by one Impulse; how all things are the cooperating Causes of all things coming to be; and what manner of spinning-together and winding-together there is.

4.41 You are a little Psyche carrying a corpse, as Epictetus used to say.[78]

4.42 Nothing is evil for things coming to be amid Transformation, just as nothing is good for things that subsist out of Transformation.

4.43 Eternity is a sort of river of things that come to be, and a violent current. For as soon as each thing has been seen, it has been carried past, and another is borne along, and that too will be carried away.

4.44 Everything that happens is as familiar and well-known as the rose in spring and the harvest fruit in summer. For such are disease, death, slander, conspiracy, and whatever delights or grieves fools.

4.45 The things that follow always arise fittingly upon the things that have preceded. For it is not like some disconnected enumeration having only what is compelled, but a rational interconnection. And just as the things which exist are arranged harmoniously together, so the things which come into being exhibit not a bare succession, but a certain wonderful kinship.

4.46 Remember always the saying of Heraclitus: that the death of earth is to become water, and the death of water is to become air, and the death of air is to become fire, and conversely.[79] And to remember also him who forgets whither the road leads. And that men are at variance with that with which they have the most continuous contact; the Reason administering the Whole. And the things which they encounter every day seem strange to them. And that one ought not to act and speak as though asleep, for even in sleep we seem to act and speak. And that one ought not to be like children of one's parents, that is, simply accepting what we have received.

4.47 Just as, if one of the Gods told you that you would die tomorrow, or at any rate by the day after tomorrow, you would not make a great matter of it being the day after tomorrow rather than tomorrow, unless you are utterly ignoble, for how small is the interval?

So too, do not think it a great matter to die many years hence rather than tomorrow.

4.48 Consider constantly how many physicians are dead after knitting their brows over their patients; how many astrologers who predicted the deaths of others as though it were a great matter; how many philosophers who expounded endlessly on death and immortality; how many great champions who killed many; how many tyrants who used their power over Psyches with terrible arrogance, as if they were immortal; how many whole cities are, so to speak, dead: Helike, Pompeii, Herculaneum, and others without number.[80]

Go over, too, those you have known, one after another. One buried another, and then was laid out. All in a short time.

In short, always look at human things as ephemeral and cheap: yesterday a drop of mucus, tomorrow pickled flesh or ashes.[81] Pass, then, this infinitesimal moment of time in accordance with Nature, and end graciously, just as an olive, having become ripe, falls, blessing the earth that bore it and giving thanks to the tree that brought it forth.

4.49 Be like the headland against which the waves constantly break: it stands firm, and around it the raging of the water is lulled to rest.

"Unlucky am I, that this has happened to me."

No, but rather: "Lucky am I that, though this has happened to me, I continue without grief, neither crushed by the Present nor fearing what is approaching." For such a thing could have happened to anyone, but not everyone would have remained without grief.

Why then is that a misfortune rather than this a good fortune? Do you call it a man's misfortune at all, when it is not a failure of man's Nature? And does something seem to you to be a failure of man's Nature if it is not contrary to the Will of his Nature?

What then is the Will?

You have learned it.

Can this that has happened prevent you from being Just, Magnanimous, Temperate, Wise, unerring, undeceived, reverent, and free? Or from any of those other qualities in whose combined presence man's Nature possesses what is properly its own?

Remember going forward, on every occasion that leads you to Distress, to use this Doctrine: it is not that this is a misfortune, but that to bear it nobly is good fortune.

4.50 A commonplace aid, yet an effective one toward the contempt of death: the recollection of those who tenaciously clung to life. What more, then, have they gained than those who died untimely?

In any case, they lie somewhere at some time or other: Cadicianus, Fabius, Julianus, Lepidus,[82] or if anyone of that sort, who carried out many to burial, and then were themselves carried out. On the whole, the interval is small, and even this, exhausted through how many things, with what sort of companions, and in what a paltry little body!

Do not then regard it as important. For look behind you at the yawning abyss of Eternity, and forward at another infinity. In the face of this, what difference is there between a three-day-old and a thrice-aged?

4.51 Always run the short way; and the short way is the way according to Nature, so as to say and do everything in the soundest manner. For such a resolve frees one from fatigue, from roundabout methods, and from all scheming and affectation.

5

Book 5

MARCUS ANTONINUS EMPEROR: To Himself. Book 5.

5.1 In the morning, when you rise unwillingly, let this thought be at hand: "I rise to do the work of a human being."

Why then am I dissatisfied, if I am going to do the things for which I was born and for which I was brought into the Cosmos? Or was I fashioned for this, to lie among the bedclothes and warm myself?

"But this is more pleasant."

Were you born for Pleasure, then? And not, in general, for undergoing and for acting? Do you not see the little plants, the little birds, the ants, the spiders, the bees, each doing its own work, each contributing to the Cosmos in its own way? And then are you unwilling to do the work of a human being? Do you not run toward what is according to your Nature?

"But one must also rest."

One must; I agree.

But Nature has given limits to this too; and to eating and drinking as well. And yet you go beyond the limits, beyond what is sufficient. But in your actions, no longer; there you stay within what is possible. For you do not love yourself, since if you did, you would love your Nature and her Will. Others who love their own crafts wear themselves out working at them, unwashed and unfed. But you honor your own Nature less than the engraver honors his art, or the dancer his art, or the miser his silver, or the vainglorious man his petty scrap of fame.

And these men, when they are devoted to their pursuits, would rather advance the things to which they are driven than eat or sleep. Yet to you, do Social Actions appear more paltry and less worthy of devotion?

5.2 How easy it is to push away and wipe clean every troubling or inappropriate Impression, and to be at once in a state of perfect calm.

5.3 Deem yourself worthy of every word and deed that is in accordance with Nature, and do not let the subsequent criticism or talk of some people distract you. If a thing is Noble to be done or said, do not think it unworthy of you. For others have their own Ruling Faculty and make use of their own Impulses. Do not look around at these things, but go straight on, following your own Nature and the Common Nature, for the path of both is one and the same.

5.4 I proceed through what is according to Nature until, having fallen, I shall rest, breathing out into this air from which I breathe daily, and falling upon this earth from which my father collected his little seed, my mother her drop of blood, and my nurse her bit of milk; from which daily, for so many years, I am fed and watered; which bears me as I tread upon it and make use of it for so many purposes.

5.5 They are unable to admire your sharpness. So be it. But there are many other things about which you cannot say, "I was not born for this." Show those things, then, which are wholly in your power: genuineness, dignity, endurance of toil, indifference to Pleasure, acceptance of one's lot, needing little, Benevolence, Freedom, Simplicity, Freedom from idle talk, and Magnanimity.

Do you not perceive how many things you are already able to offer, things for which you have no excuse of natural incapacity or unsuitability, and yet you still remain down voluntarily? Or are you compelled to grumble, to be stingy, to flatter, to blame your poor little body, to curry favor, to boast, and to be so tossed about in your Psyche; all because you are naturally ill-constituted?

No, by the Gods! You could have been rid of these long ago. Only this much: if indeed you are to be faulted, it is for being rather slow and harder to follow in comprehension; and even this must be practiced, neither overlooking it nor taking pleasure in sluggishness.

5.6 One man, when he has done a kindness for someone, is ready to reckon the favor to his own account. Another is not ready to do this, but nonetheless within himself he thinks of the other as a debtor, and he is well aware of what he has done. But a third, in a way, does not even know what he has done, but is like a vine that has borne a cluster of grapes and seeks nothing more after it has once borne its own fruit. A horse that has run, a dog that has tracked, a bee that has made honey, and a man who has done good does not proclaim it, but moves on to another act, as a vine moves on to bear its cluster again in season.

"Therefore, one must be among those who do these things without being aware of it?"

"Yes. But one must be aware of this very thing; for," he says, "it is characteristic of the Social being to perceive that he is acting socially, and by Zeus, to want his fellow to perceive it too."

"What you say is true, but you mistake what is now being said. Because of this, you will be one of those whom I mentioned before; for they too are led astray by a certain rational plausibility. But if you wish to understand what is actually being said, do not fear that you will thereby omit any Social Work."

5.7 A prayer of the Athenians: "Rain, rain, O dear Zeus, upon the plowland of the Athenians and the plains."

Either do not pray at all, or pray like this: so simply and freely.

5.8 Consider what is meant by the saying that: "Asclepius prescribed for this man horse-riding, or cold baths, or walking barefoot."[83]

Such also is this: "the Nature of the Whole prescribed for this man a disease, or maiming, or loss, or anything else of that sort."

For in the first case, "prescribed" signifies something like this: he ordered this for this man as suitable for health. And here too, that which happens to each has been ordered somehow for him as fitting with respect to Fate.

For we say that things "happen" to us, just as craftsmen speak of squared stones in walls or in the pyramids "happening to fit together," fitting together with one another in a particular arrangement. For altogether there is one harmony. And just as the Cosmos is completed out of all Bodies to be such a Body, so Fate is completed out of all Causes to be such a Cause.

Even those who are complete laymen understand what I say. For they say: "It brought this to him." Therefore, this was brought to this man, and this was prescribed to this man. Let us accept these things, then, as those things which Asclepius prescribes. For many, at any rate, even among his prescriptions are harsh; but we welcome them with the hope of health.

Let the accomplishment and completion of the things decreed by Common Nature seem to you something like your own health. And thus welcome everything that happens, even if it seems rather harsh, because it leads you there: to the health of the Cosmos and the prosperous course and good fortune of Zeus. For Nature would not have brought this to anyone if it were not advantageous to the Whole. For neither does any nature whatsoever bring anything that is not suitable to that which is governed by it.

Therefore, for two reasons you must cherish what happens to you. For one, that it happened to you, and was prescribed to you, and was related to you in some way from above, spun together from the most ancient Causes. For the other, that for the One governing the Whole, even that which comes individually to each person is a Cause of His welfare and completion, and by Zeus, of His very continuance.

For the intact Whole is maimed if you sever anything whatsoever from the connection and continuity, of the Causes no less than of the parts. And you do sever it, as far as it depends on you, whenever you are discontented, and in a way, you destroy it.

5.9 Do not be disgusted, nor give up, nor lose heart, if acting from right Principles in all things does not become second nature to you. But whenever you are knocked off course, come back again, and take satisfaction if the majority of your actions are worthier of a human being; and love that to which you return.

And do not return to Philosophy as to a schoolmaster, but as those with sore eyes turn to the sponge and the egg,[84] or as another turns to a poultice or a fomentation. In this way, you will not be making a show of obeying Reason, but will rest upon it.

Remember that Philosophy wills only what your Nature wills; but you wanted something else that was not according to Nature. For what is more pleasant than these? For does not Pleasure trip you up for this very reason?

But see if Magnanimity, Freedom, Simplicity, Equanimity, and Piety are not more pleasant. For what is more pleasant than Practical Wisdom itself, when you reflect on the unerring and smooth-flowing quality in all things of the faculty of comprehension and knowledge?

5.10 Things are in a manner so veiled that many philosophers, and not insignificant ones, believed them to be entirely incomprehensible. Even to the Stoics themselves, they merely seem difficult to comprehend. And every Assent of ours is subject to change, for where is the person who never changes?

Turn, then, to the objects themselves, and see how short-lived and worthless they are: capable of being possessed by a catamite or a prostitute,[85] or a robber. Then consider the characters of your associates; it is hard to endure even the most agreeable of them, not to mention that a man can hardly bear even himself.

In such gloom and filth, in such a flux of Substance and time, of motion and things moved, I cannot even conceive what there is that could be highly valued or earnestly pursued. On the contrary, one must console oneself while waiting for the natural Dissolution, and not be vexed at the delay, but find rest in these considerations alone:

First, that nothing will happen to me which is not in accordance with the Nature of the Whole.

Second, that it is in my power to do nothing contrary to my own God and Daimon. For there is no one who can compel me to transgress this.

5.11 For what purpose am I now using my own Psyche? On every occasion, ask this of yourself and examine:

"What do I have now in this part of me which they call the Ruling Faculty? And what sort of Psyche do I have right now? That of a child? That of a youth? That of a petty woman?[86] That of a tyrant? That of cattle? That of a wild beast?"

5.12 What sort of things those are which the many consider good, you can grasp even from this. For if someone were to conceive of certain things as truly good, such as Practical Wisdom, Temperance, Justice, and Courage, having preconceived these, he could no longer listen to [the comic phrase]; on account of the goods.[87]

But the things that appear good to the many, having preconceived those, one will listen to and easily accept as fittingly said what was spoken by the comic poet. This is how even the multitude perceives the difference. For otherwise, the first would not offend and be rejected, while the second, about wealth and the windfalls of luxury or fame, we would accept as apt and witty.

Proceed, then, and ask: 'Should those things be honored and considered good?'

Of which things, when preconceived, one could fittingly add: 'Because of his abundance, he has nowhere to shit.'[88]

5.13 I am composed of the Causal and the Material; and neither of these will perish into non-being, any more than it came into existence from non-existence. Every part of me will be assigned into some part of the Cosmos by Transformation, and that in turn will be transformed into another part of the Cosmos, and so on to infinity. Through the very same process of

Transformation I myself came into being, as did those who begat me, and so on backward through another infinity. One may perhaps still speak in this way even if the Cosmos is governed according to finite, recurring cycles.

5.14 Reason and the Art of Reasoning are faculties sufficient for themselves and their own works. They start from their own first principle and proceed to their appointed Goal. Such actions are therefore called "Right Actions,"[89] from the word that signifies the rightness of their path.

5.15 None of these things should be called proper to a human being which do not befit him insofar as he is a human being. They are not demanded of him, nor does Human Nature promise them, nor are they perfections of Human Nature. Therefore neither the end of a human being, nor the completion of that end, the Good, lies in these things.

Since, if any of these things did befit a human being, it would not befit him to despise them and set himself against them; nor would a man be praiseworthy who made himself free from the need of them; nor would the man deficient in any of them be good, if indeed these were goods. But as it is, the more a man removes these and similar things from himself, or, when they are taken away, endures it, the more he is good.

5.16 Whatever things you frequently picture to yourself, of such a sort your Mind will be; for the Psyche is dyed by its Impressions.

Dye it, therefore, with a continuous stream of such Impressions as these: where it is possible to live, it is possible to live well; but it is possible to live in a palace; therefore, it is possible to live well in a palace.

And again: each thing has been constructed for a purpose, and it is drawn toward that for which it was constructed. In that toward which it is drawn lies its end. And where the end is, there too is the advantage and the Good of each thing. The Good for a Rational Animal, therefore, is Community. For we have long since been shown to be born for Community.

Or was it not evident that inferior things exist for the sake of the superior, and the superior for one another?

But living things are superior to non-living, and Rational beings are superior to the merely living.

5.17 To pursue what is impossible is madness; and it is impossible for the wicked not to do such things.

5.18 Nothing befalls anyone that he is not naturally fitted to bear. The same things happen to another, and he, either through ignorance of what has happened or by displaying Magnanimity, stands firm and remains unharmed. It is a terrible thing, then, that ignorance and self-satisfaction should be stronger than Practical Wisdom.

5.19 Things themselves do not touch the Psyche in any way; they have no entry to the Psyche, nor can they turn or move it. The Psyche alone turns and moves itself, and whatever Judgments it deems worthy of itself, such it makes the things that present themselves to it.

5.20 In one respect, man is the thing most kindred to us, insofar as we must do them good and bear with them. But insofar as some stand in the way of our proper actions, man becomes for me one of the Indifferent things, no less than the sun, the wind, or a wild beast. By these, some action may be impeded, but they are no impediments to my Impulse and Disposition, because of Reservation and redirection. For the Mind converts and transposes every obstacle to action into what advances the purpose: what restrains a work becomes serviceable for the work, and what obstructs a road becomes advantageous for the road.

5.21 Honor what is strongest in the Cosmos; it is that which uses all things and governs all things. And likewise, honor what is strongest in yourself; for it is of the same kind. For in your case too, it is that which uses the other things, and your life is governed by it.

5.22 That which does no harm to the City does no harm to the Citizen. Upon every Impression of having been harmed, apply this rule: if the City is not harmed by this, then I am not harmed either. But if the City is harmed, one must not be angry with the one who harms it, but show him what he has overlooked.

5.23 Reflect often on the swiftness of the passing and withdrawal of all things that exist and come into being. For Substance is like a river in perpetual flow, and actions are in constant Transformation, and Causes in countless transformations; almost nothing stands still, even what is near at hand. And consider the boundless vastness of the past and the future, in which all things vanish. How foolish, then, is the one who is puffed up amid such things, or is pulled about, or wails as though troubled by something lasting!

5.24 Remember the whole of Substance, of which you have the smallest share; and the whole of Eternity, of which a brief and infinitesimal interval has been marked off for you; and the whole of Fate, and how small your part in it is.

5.25 Does another commit some wrong against me?

Let him see to it. He has his own disposition and his own activity. I now have what Common Nature wills me to have, and I do what my own Nature wills me to do.

5.26 Let the Ruling Faculty remain unaltered by the smooth or rough motions in the flesh. Let it not be commingled with them, but let it circumscribe itself and confine those affections to the bodily parts. But when these are transmitted to the Mind through Sympathy, as happens in a unified body, then one must not try to resist the sensation, since it is natural; but let the Ruling Faculty not of itself add the Judgment that it is something good or bad.

5.27 "To live with the Gods." And he lives with the Gods who constantly shows them a Psyche that is satisfied with its assigned portion, and that does all that the Daimon wishes, which Zeus has given to every man as his guardian and guide, a fragment of Himself. And this is each man's Intellect and Reason.

5.28 Are you angry with the man who stinks of sweat? Are you angry with the man whose breath is foul? What can he do about it?

He has such a mouth, he has such armpits; it is necessary that such an odor comes from such sources.

"But the man has Reason," one says, "and is capable, if he applies himself, of perceiving where he errs."

Good for you!

Therefore you too have Reason: by your Rational Disposition move his Rational Disposition; show him, remind him. For if he heeds you, you will cure him, and there will be no need for anger. Neither tragic actor nor whore.

5.29 As you intend to live once you depart, so it is possible to live here. But if they do not allow it, then depart from life; yet in such a way as one suffering nothing bad. There is smoke, and I depart.[90]

Why do you think it a great matter?

But as long as no such thing drives me out, I remain free, and no one will prevent me from doing what I wish; and I wish to live according to the Nature of a Rational and Social Animal.

5.30 The Intellect of the Whole is Social. At any rate, it has made the inferior things for the sake of the superior, and it has fitted the superior to one another. You see how it has subordinated, coordinated, assigned to everything its proper share, and brought the most excellent beings into concord with one another.

5.31 How have you conducted yourself until now toward Gods, parents, brothers, wife, children, teachers, tutors, friends, relatives, household slaves?

Consider whether toward all of them you can say to this very day: 'Neither to have done anything outrageous to anyone by deed, nor to have said anything [so].'

And remember through what things you have passed and what you have had the strength to endure; that the story of your life is already complete and your service is fulfilled. How many beautiful things you have seen, how many pleasures and pains you have disdained, how many glories you have disregarded, and toward how many ungrateful people you have shown yourself gracious.

5.32 Why do unskilled and ignorant Psyches confound one who is skilled and knowledgeable?

What Psyche, then, is skilled and knowledgeable?

The one that knows the beginning and the end, and the Reason that pervades the whole of Substance and administers the All throughout all Eternity according to fixed cycles.

5.33 You will very soon be ashes or a skeleton, and a name, or not even a name; and the name is a sound and an echo. The things much-prized in life are empty, rotten, and trivial: little dogs biting one another, squabbling children, laughing one moment and weeping the next. But Trust, Reverence, Justice, and Truth have "fled from the broad-wayed earth to Olympus."[91]

What, then, still keeps you here?

The objects of sense are changeable and unstable, the senses themselves are dim and easily receiving false Impressions, the little Psyche itself is a mere Exhalation from blood, and to be well-regarded among such people is an empty thing.

What then?

Await graciously either Extinction or Transition.

And until that moment arrives, what is sufficient?

What else but to revere and praise the Gods, to do good to men, to bear with them and to abstain. Whatever is within the bounds of your little flesh and your little Pneuma, remember that these are neither yours nor in your power.

5.34 You can always flow well in life, if you can travel the right path, if you can judge and act along the right way. These two things are common to the Psyche of God, the Psyche of humans, and that of every Rational Animal: not to be hindered by another, and to hold the Good in a just disposition and action, and to let Desire end there.

5.35 If this is neither my own Vice nor an action proceeding from my Vice, and if the Common Good is not harmed, why am I troubled about it? And what is the harm to the Common Good?

5.36 Do not be wholly carried away by the Impression, but help as far as your power allows and according to merit, even if they suffer loss in things Indifferent; do not, however, imagine this to be harm, for that is a bad habit. But just as the old man, on leaving, asked back for his ward's spinning top, remembering that it was a top, so act in this case also.[92] For what are you becoming, prattling upon the podium?[93]

O man, have you forgotten what these things were?

"Yes, but to these people they are matters of intense pursuit."

Should you therefore also become a fool?

5.37 I was once, in whatever situation I found myself, a fortunate man. But "fortunate" means having assigned yourself a good portion. And good portions are: good inclinations of the Psyche, good Impulses, good actions.

6

Book 6

MARCUS ANTONINUS EMPEROR: To Himself. Book 6.

6.1 The Substance of the Whole is compliant and adaptable, and the Reason that governs it has in itself no Cause for doing Vice, for it has no malice, does no evil, and nothing is harmed by it. All things are brought into being and are accomplished according to it.

6.2 Let it make no difference to you whether, shivering or warm, you do what is fitting; and whether drowsy or well-rested; and whether spoken ill of or praised; and whether dying or doing something else. For dying too is one of the acts of life; it is sufficient, therefore, even in this act, to manage the Present well.

6.3 Look within. Let neither the particular quality nor the worth of any thing escape you.

6.4 All underlying things rapidly transform, and will either be resolved into vapor if Substance is unified, or be scattered.

6.5 The governing Reason knows how it is disposed, what it does, and upon what Matter.

6.6 The best retaliation is not to become like them.

6.7 Take pleasure and rest in one thing: passing from one Social act to another Social act, with the remembrance of God.

6.8 The Ruling Faculty is that which rouses itself and directs itself, making itself whatever it wills to be, and making all that happens appear to it as it wills.

6.9 Each thing is accomplished according to the Nature of the Whole. For it is not according to any other Nature: either one containing it from without, or contained within it, or existing apart from it.

6.10 Either it is a muddle, a mutual entanglement and dispersal, or it is unity, order, and Providence.

If the former, why do I desire to linger in a random compound and such a confused mass? Why should I care about anything other than how I shall eventually become earth? Why am I troubled?

For dispersal will come upon me no matter what I do. But if the latter is the case, I revere, I stand firm, and I trust in the Governor.

6.11 When you are compelled by circumstances, as it were, to be thrown into disorder, return to yourself quickly, and do not step outside the rhythm more than is necessary. For you will be more in command of the harmony by constantly returning to it.

6.12 If you had a stepmother and a mother at the same time, you would serve your stepmother, and yet your return to your mother would be constant. Such are the Court and Philosophy to you now. Return to her often and find your rest in her, she through whom the affairs of the court seem tolerable to you, and you tolerable to them.

6.13 What a thing it is to form an Impression concerning dishes and such edible things: this is the corpse of a fish, that the corpse of a bird or a pig; and again, that Falernian wine[94] is merely the little juice of a grape-cluster, and that purple-bordered toga is but the little hairs of a sheep dyed with the gore of a shellfish; and, concerning sexual intercourse, that it is the friction of entrails and, with a certain spasm, the ejection of a little snot.

Such indeed are these Impressions, reaching the things themselves and penetrating through them, so as to see what sort of things they really are. Thus you must do throughout your whole life; and where things appear most worthy of belief, strip them naked and behold their cheapness, and strip away the narrative by which they pride themselves. For vanity is a terrible deceiver, and when you think you are most occupied with serious matters, then you are most bewitched by it.

See, then, what Crates says about Xenocrates himself.[95]

6.14 Most things that the masses admire can be referred to the most general categories: things held together by Cohesion or by Nature, such as stones, wood, fig trees, vines, olives. But those admired by the slightly more refined are referred to things held together by Psyche, such as flocks of sheep and herds of cattle. And those by the still more cultivated, to things held together by Rational Psyche, not, however, the Universal Rational Psyche, but only insofar as it is skilled in craft or otherwise clever, or merely amounts to the possession of a multitude of slaves.[96]

But he who honors the Rational Psyche, the Universal and Civic one, no longer pays attention to any of those other things. Above all, he preserves his own Psyche rationally and socially disposed and so acting, and cooperates with his own kind toward this end.

6.15 Some things hasten to come into being, and others hasten to have already become; and of that which is coming into existence, some part is already extinguished. Flowings and Alterations renew the Cosmos constantly, just as the uninterrupted course of time provides the infinite Eternity, ever new. In this river, then, what could one value among the things rushing past, when it is not possible to stand upon any of them?

It is as if one should begin to grow fond of one of the little birds flying past, but it has already gone from sight. For such indeed is the very life of each person: like the exhalation from the blood and the drawing of breath from the air. For just as it is to draw in the air once and give it back, which we do at every moment, so too is it to give back the whole breathing faculty to that place from where you first drew it: this faculty which you acquired when you were born yesterday or the day before.

6.16 It is of no value to breathe outward like plants, or to breathe like cattle and wild beasts, or to be molded according to Impression, or to be jerked by the puppet-strings of Impulse, or to herd together, or to be nourished. For this last is similar to excreting the residues of food.

What then is valuable? The applause of hands?

No. Therefore, not even the applause of tongues; for the praises of the multitude are merely the applause of tongues. So you have cast away little glory too.

What remains valuable?

It seems to me: to move and to be restrained according to your own proper Constitution, the end toward which both diligent practices and the arts lead. For every art aims at this: that the thing fashioned should be well suited for the work for which it was fashioned. The gardener and the one tending the vine, the colt-breaker and the one tending the dog: all seek this.

And toward what do the arts of tutoring and of teaching hasten?

Toward this end. Here then is the value. And if this be well with you, you will seek to acquire none of the other things. But if you do not cease valuing many other things, you will be neither free, nor self-sufficient, nor free from Passions. For it is necessary that you be envious and jealous, and suspicious of those who can take those things away, and plot against those who possess what is valued by you. Altogether, it is necessary for one who lacks any of those things to be in turmoil, and furthermore to blame the Gods for many things. But the reverence and honor for your own Mind makes you pleasing to yourself, and harmonious with your companions, and consonant with the Gods, that is, praising whatever they assign and have ordained.

6.17 Above, below, in a circle: the movements of the Elements. But the movement of Virtue is in none of these; it is something more divine, and going forward by a path hard to conceive, it prospers.

6.18 What sort of thing they do! They are unwilling to praise their contemporaries who live among them, yet they themselves set great store on being praised by posterity, by men they have never seen and never will see. This is close to being troubled because earlier generations did not also make praising[97] remarks about you.

6.19 Do not think that because a thing is hard for you to achieve, it is impossible for any man. Rather, if a thing is possible and proper for a man, consider it to be within your own reach also.

6.20 In the gymnasium, someone scratches us with his nails, or lunging with his head, delivers a blow; yet we do not make a show of it, nor are we offended, nor do we suspect him afterward of plotting against us. We are on our guard, it is true, but not as against an enemy or with suspicion; we simply keep our distance with a benevolent avoidance.

Let it be so in the other parts of life. Let us overlook many things done by those who are, as it were, our sparring partners. For it is possible, as I have said, to keep our distance without suspicion or hatred.

6.21 If anyone can refute me and prove to me that I am wrong in judgment or deed, I will gladly change. For I seek the Truth, by which no one was ever harmed. But one is harmed who persists in one's own self-deception and ignorance.

6.22 I perform my Appropriate Actions; other things do not distract me. For they are either without Psyche, or irrational, or have lost their way and are ignorant of the path.

6.23 As for irrational animals, things in general, and underlying substances, make use of them with Magnanimity and freely, since you have Reason and they lack Reason. But as for men, who do have Reason, treat them communally. In all things, call upon the Gods. And do not trouble yourself about how long you will do this, for even three hours spent in this way are sufficient.

6.24 Alexander of Macedon and his mule-tender, upon death, came to the same state: they were either received back into the same Seminal Reasons of the Cosmos, or scattered alike into Atoms.

6.25 Consider how many things, both of Body and of Psyche, are happening in each of us in the same brief instant of time; and so you will not wonder that far more things (indeed, all things that come to be) subsist together in that One and Universal Whole which we call the Cosmos.

6.26 If someone should ask you how the name Antoninus is spelled, would you strain to pronounce each letter? Then if they grow angry, will you become angry in return? Will you not calmly proceed, enumerating each letter?

So too here in life, remember that every Appropriate Action is composed of a definite number of steps. You must observe these and, without becoming disturbed or vexed at those who are vexed with you, accomplish the task at hand by the proper path.

6.27 How cruel it is not to permit men to rush toward what appears to them suitable and beneficial!

Yet, in a way, you do not allow them to do this when you become indignant that they err. For they are surely drawn to these things as being appropriate and beneficial to them.

"But that is not so."

Therefore, teach and show without being indignant.

6.28 Death: a rest from the reactive impact of sensation, from the jerking of Impulse, from the excursions of the Mind, and from service to the flesh.

6.29 It is a shameful thing that the Psyche should give up first in this life, when the Body has not.

6.30 Take care that you are not *Caesarized*,[98] that you are not dyed with that dye, for it happens. Keep yourself, therefore, simple, good, pure, serious, unadorned, a friend of the Just, pious, kind, affectionate, and strong for the works that are fitting. Strive to remain such as Philosophy wished to make you. Revere the Gods, and save human beings. Life is short. The one fruit of this earthly life is a holy disposition and Social acts.

In all things, be as a disciple of Antoninus.[99] His vigor in matters done according to Reason, his evenness in all things, his Piety, the serenity of his face, his sweetness, his freedom from vainglory, and his eagerness for the apprehension of things. Remember how he would let nothing pass without first looking into it carefully and understanding it clearly; how he tolerated those who blamed him unjustly, without blaming them in return; how he was never hurried in anything; how he would not entertain slander; how exact an examiner he was of characters and actions; not reproachful, not timid, not suspicious, not a sophist. Remember how content he was with little; in housing, bedding, clothes, food, and servants; how hard-working and patient he was; how he could remain in the same place until evening, and due to his simple diet had no need to excrete waste except at his customary hour. Remember his firmness and uniformity in friendship; his tolerance of those who frankly opposed his opinions, and his delight if anyone showed him something better; and how he worshipped the Gods without superstition. Remember all this, so that your last hour may find you with as clear a conscience as his.

6.31 Sober up and call yourself back, and once you have awoken from sleep and realized that it was only dreams that troubled you, look upon these things, now awake, as you looked upon those.

6.32 I am composed of a little Body and a Psyche. To the little Body, all things are Indifferent, for it cannot differentiate. To the Mind, all things are Indifferent that are not its own activities; and all of its own activities are in its power. And of these, it is concerned only with the Present; for its future and past activities are themselves already Indifferent.

6.33 Toil is not contrary to Nature for the hand or the foot, so long as the foot does the work of a foot and the hand the work of a hand. So too for a human, as a human, toil is not contrary to Nature, so long as he does the work of a human. And if it is not contrary to his Nature, it is not an evil for him.

6.34 Look at what pleasures have been enjoyed by robbers, catamites, patricides, and tyrants!

6.35 Do you not see how common craftsmen, though they accommodate themselves to the unskilled up to a point, still hold to the Reason of their art and will not depart from it? Is it not outrageous if the architect and the doctor show more reverence for the Reason of their own arts than a man does for his own Reason, which he shares with the Gods?

6.36 Asia and Europe are corners of the Cosmos; the whole sea, a drop in the Cosmos; Mount Athos, a tiny clod of the Cosmos; all present time is a point in Eternity. All things are small, easily altered, and vanishing. All things come from there, having originated from the Common Ruling Faculty, or by consequence. The lion's gaping jaws, poison, and every malignity, like thorns, like filth, are by-products of what is grand and beautiful. Do not, then, imagine these to be alien to that which you revere, but reflect upon the source of all things.

6.37 He who has seen the present has seen all things: both whatever has come to be from Eternity and whatever will be unto Infinity. For all things are of the same kind and of the same form.

6.38 Reflect often on the connection of all things in the Cosmos and their relation to one another. For in a way, all things are interwoven, and therefore all things are friendly to one another. For one thing is in succession to another, because of the tensional motion, the common breath, and the unity of Substance.

6.39 Adapt yourself to the things that have been assigned to you; and the people with whom you have been cast together, truly love them.

6.40 An instrument, a tool, any utensil is in a good state if it does the work for which it was made, even though its maker is absent. But in things held together by Nature, the constructing power that made them is present within and remains. Therefore, you must revere it all the more, and consider that if you hold yourself and conduct yourself according to its will, all things are in accord with Intellect for you. In this way also, for the All, its own things are according to Intellect.

6.41 Whatever among things outside your Moral Will you establish as good or evil for yourself, it must follow that if you fall into such an evil or fail to obtain such a good, you will blame the Gods and hate the humans who are the cause, or suspected to be the cause, of your failure or misfortune. Indeed, we commit many injustices because of our making such distinctions. But if we deem only those things to be good or evil which are in our own power, there is no reason left either to accuse God or to stand as an enemy to humans.

6.42 We are all working together toward one result, some knowingly and with full comprehension, others without awareness. Just as Heraclitus, I think, says that even those who are asleep are workers and collaborators in what happens in the Cosmos. One cooperates in one way, another in another, and abundantly so, even the one who finds fault, who tries to resist and destroy what is happening. For the Cosmos has need even of such a person.

Consider, then, among which group you will place yourself. For the One Administering the Whole will certainly make good use of you and will receive you into the ranks of his collaborators. But see that you do not become such a part as the cheap and ridiculous verse in the play that Chrysippus mentions.[100]

6.43 Does the Sun presume to do the work of the rain, or Asclepius the work of the Fruit-Bearer [Demeter]?[101] And what of each of the stars? Are they not different, yet work together for the same end?

6.44 If the Gods have deliberated about me and about what ought to happen to me, they have deliberated well. For a God without counsel is hard even to imagine. And for what Cause would they be inclined to do me harm? For what would accrue to them, or to the Common Good, for which they exercise the greatest Providence, from this? But if they have not deliberated about me individually, they have certainly deliberated about the Common Good, and the things that happen as a consequence of that, I ought to welcome and cherish.

But if they deliberate about nothing (which it is impious to believe) or else let us neither sacrifice, nor pray, nor swear oaths, nor do any of the other things we do, believing the Gods to be present and living with us. If, I say, they deliberate about nothing concerning us, it is permitted to me to deliberate about myself, and mine is the inquiry concerning what is advantageous. And that is useful to each person which is conformable to his own Constitution and Nature. My Nature is Rational and Civic. My city and fatherland, as Antoninus, is Rome; as a human being, it is the Cosmos. Therefore, only what is useful to these cities is good for me.

6.45 Whatever happens to the individual is beneficial to the Whole. This suffices. But if you observe carefully, you will generally see this also: what is beneficial for one man is beneficial also for other men. But let 'beneficial' here be taken in its broader sense, as referring to Indifferents.

6.46 Just as the shows in the amphitheater and such places weary you, always the same things being seen, and the sameness makes the spectacle tiresome, so too must you experience this with the whole of life. For all things, from top to bottom, are the same and from the same sources. How long, then?

6.47 Think constantly of all sorts of men who have died, of every kind of profession and every nation, so that your thought reaches down even to Philistion and Phoebus and Origanion.[102]

Now pass on to the other tribes. To that place we too must depart, where there are so many clever orators, so many revered philosophers, Heraclitus, Pythagoras, Socrates, so many heroes of former times, and after them so many generals and tyrants.

Besides these: Eudoxus, Hipparchus, Archimedes, and other sharp, great-minded, hard-working, resourceful, and stubborn natures, even mockers of the very perishable and ephemeral life of men, such as Menippus and all such types.[103] Concerning all these, reflect that they have long been laid to rest.

What then is so terrible about that for them?

And what of those not even named at all?

One thing here is of great value: to pass through life with Truth and Justice, and with kindness even toward liars and the unjust.

6.48 When you wish to gladden yourself, call to mind the excellent qualities of those who live with you: for instance, the energy of one, the modesty of another, the generosity of a third, and something else of yet another. For nothing so delights as the likenesses of the Virtues manifesting themselves in the characters of those who live alongside us, and converging all together as much as possible. Therefore, one must keep them ready to hand.

6.49 Are you annoyed because you weigh only so many pounds and not three hundred? So also that you must live only so many years and not more?

For just as you are content with the portion of Substance allotted to you, so you should be with Time.

6.50 Try to persuade them. But act, even against their will, when the Reason of Justice so demands. If, however, someone opposes you by force, then turn to contentment and freedom from Distress, and use the obstacle to practice another Virtue. Remember that your Impulse was conditional, and that you did not aim at the impossible. What then did you aim for?

To have such an Impulse. And this you have achieved; what we set out to do is accomplished.

6.51 The lover of glory considers another's action to be his own good; the lover of pleasure, his own experience; but the one who has Intellect considers his own action to be his good.

6.52 It is in your power, concerning this thing, to form no assumption, and not to trouble the Psyche. For the things themselves have no nature capable of creating our Judgments.

6.53 Accustom yourself not to be inattentive to what another says, and as far as possible, enter into his Psyche.

6.54 What is not beneficial for the swarm is not beneficial for the bee.

6.55 If the sailors spoke ill of the helmsman, or the sick of the doctor, would he attend to anything other than how to secure the safety of those on board, or the health of those under his care?

6.56 How many of those with whom I entered the Cosmos have already exited?

6.57 To the jaundiced, honey tastes bitter; to those bitten by a rabid dog, water is terrifying; to little boys, a ball is a fine thing.

Why, then, am I angry?

Does it seem to you that delusion is less powerful than bile in the jaundiced or venom in the rabid?

6.58 No one can prevent you from living according to the Reason of your own Nature; nothing will happen to you contrary to the Reason of Common Nature.

6.59 What kind of people are those whom they wish to please, and through what Passions, and through what actions?

How swiftly Eternity will bury all things, and how many it has buried already.

7

Book 7

MARCUS ANTONINUS EMPEROR: To Himself. Book 7.

7.1 What is Vice?

It is that which you have seen often. And for every occurrence, have this ready: "It is that which you have seen often."

Everywhere, up and down, you will find the same things, of which the ancient histories, the middle ones, and the recent are full; and of which cities and houses are full now. There is nothing new. All things are both familiar and short-lived.

7.2 How can convictions die, unless the Impressions corresponding to them are extinguished?

It is in your power to rekindle these continually.

I am able to form the proper judgment about this; if I am able, why am I disturbed?

The things outside my Mind are absolutely nothing to my Mind. Learn this, and you stand upright. It is in your power to come back to life. Look at things again as you used to look at them; for in this lies the coming back to life.

7.3 The empty striving of a procession, plays on a stage, flocks, herds, spear-combats, a little bone thrown to little dogs, a crumb cast into the fish ponds, the hardships and burdens of ants, the scurrying of startled little mice, puppets pulled by strings. It is necessary, then, to stand among these things kindly and without snorting with pride; but to observe that each person is worth as much as the things about which he is zealous are worth.

7.4 One must follow word-by-word what is being said, and in every Impulse to follow what is happening. Regarding the one, one must see immediately the target toward which it is directed; regarding the other, one must watch carefully for the meaning.

7.5 Is my Mind sufficient for this or not?

If it is sufficient, I use it for the work as a tool provided by the Nature of the Whole. But if it is not sufficient, I either yield the work to one who is able to complete it better (unless it is otherwise my duty) or I do it as best I can, taking to my aid one who, with the guidance of my Ruling Faculty, can accomplish what is currently timely and useful for the Community. For whatever I do, whether by myself or with another, ought to be directed to that alone which is useful and suitable to the Community.

7.6 How many of those once celebrated are already given over to oblivion? And how many who sang their praises are already long gone?

7.7 Do not be ashamed to be helped. For your task is to accomplish what has been set before you, like a soldier in an assault on a wall.

What, then, if you are lame and cannot scale the battlement alone, but can do so with the help of another?

7.8 Do not let the future disturb you. For you will come to them, if need be, carrying the same Reason which you now use for present things.

7.9 All things are intertwined with one another, and the bond is sacred;

and scarcely anything is alien to anything else, for they have been arranged together and together adorn the same Cosmos. For there is one Cosmos out of all things, and one God through all things, and one Substance, and one Law, one Reason common to all Intellectual Animals, and one Truth, if indeed there is also one Perfection of beings of the same stock, animals partaking of the same Reason.

7.10 All Material things vanish most swiftly into the Substance of the Whole; and every Cause is most swiftly taken back into the Reason of the Whole; and the memory of all things is most swiftly buried in Eternity.

7.11 For the Rational Animal, the same act is according to Nature and according to Reason.

7.12 Stand upright, not held upright.

7.13 Just as the limbs of the body are in a united organism, so Rational beings, though in separate bodies, stand in the same relation: constituted for a single cooperation. This thought will strike you more sharply if you say to yourself often: "I am a limb of the system of Rational beings." But if by using the letter Rho[104] you say you are a 'part', you do not yet love human beings from the heart; doing good does not yet delight you with cognitive certainty; you still do it merely as the right thing to do, not yet as doing good for yourself.

7.14 Let whatever wishes befall from outside upon those parts able to suffer from this occurrence. For those parts, if they wish, may complain. But I, unless I judge what has happened to be an evil, have not yet been harmed. And it is in my power not to judge it so.

7.15 Whatever anyone does or says, I must be good. Just as if gold, or an emerald, or purple were always saying: "Whatever anyone does or says, I must be an emerald and keep my own color."

7.16 The Ruling Faculty does not disturb itself; I mean, for example, it does not frighten itself into Desire. But if any other thing is able to frighten it or pain it, let it do so. For the Faculty itself will not turn itself by its own assumptions into such transformations. Let the little Body take care, if it can, that it not suffer anything; and if it suffers, let it say so. But the little Psyche, the one that fears, the one that grieves, the one that forms opinions about these things, will suffer nothing, for you will not lead it into such a judgment. The Ruling Faculty is without need, insofar as it depends on itself, unless it makes itself needy. And likewise it is untroubled and unimpeded, unless it troubles and impedes itself.

7.17 Happiness is a good Daimon, or a good Ruling Faculty. What are you doing here, O Impression? Go away, by the Gods, just as you came; for I do not need you. You came according to your ancient habit. I am not angry with you; just go away.

7.18 Does someone fear Transformation? But what can come into being without Transformation? What is dearer or more familiar to the Nature of the Whole? Can you yourself take a hot bath unless the wood undergoes a Transformation? Can you be nourished unless your food undergoes a Transformation? And can anything else useful be accomplished without Transformation? Do you not see, then, that your own Transformation is of the same kind, and equally necessary to the Nature of the Whole?

7.19 Through the Substance of the Whole, as through a rushing torrent, all bodies pass, grown together with the Whole and cooperating with it, as our own limbs do with one another. How many a Chrysippus, how many a Socrates, how many an Epictetus has Eternity already swallowed up! Let the same thought strike you regarding every man and every thing.

7.20 One thing alone distracts me: that I not do something which the Constitution of man does not wish, or in the way it does not wish, or what it does not wish right now.

7.21 Near is your oblivion of all things; and near is the oblivion of you by all things.

7.22 It is a peculiarity of man to love even those who transgress. And this happens if it occurs to you that they are your kinsmen, and that they err through ignorance and involuntarily, and that soon both of you will be dead; and above all, that he has not harmed you; for he has not made your Ruling Faculty worse than it was before.

7.23 The Nature of the Whole, from the Substance of the Whole as from wax, now molds a little horse; and when she has broken this up she uses that Material for a little tree; then for a little manikin; then for something else. And each of these subsists for a very short time. But there is nothing dreadful about the dismantling of the box, any more than there was anything good about the putting of it together.

7.24 A scowling face is very contrary to Nature. When it is assumed often enough, the natural bearing of the face dies away, or is eventually extinguished so that it can never be rekindled at all. Try to grasp this very point: that it is contrary to Reason. For if the perception of doing wrong is also lost, what purpose is there left for living?

7.25 All things you see, the Nature which governs the Whole will soon transform and will make other things from their Substance, and again other things from the Substance of those, so that the Cosmos may always be young.

7.26 When someone wrongs you, immediately consider what opinion of good or evil he had when he did it. For when you see this, you will pity him, and you will neither be surprised at him nor be angry. For you yourself either still hold the same opinion as he does regarding what is "good," or something similar. You must therefore make allowance for him. But if you no longer hold such things to be good or evil, you will more easily be kind to the one who sees wrongly.

7.27 Do not think of things that are absent as if they were already present; but of the things that are present, select the most favorable, and remind yourself how eagerly you would have sought them if they were not present. At the same time, however, take care lest by delighting in them this way you become so accustomed to valuing them that, if they were ever not to be there, you would be disturbed.

7.28 Contract into yourself. The Rational Ruling Faculty has this Nature: to be content with itself when it acts justly, and by doing so, to possess calm.

7.29 Wipe out the Impression. Stop the jerking of puppet-strings. Circumscribe the present moment. Recognize what is happening to you or to another. Divide and separate the subject into the Causal and the Material. Think upon your last hour. Let the wrong done by another remain where the wrong was done.

7.30 Extend your thinking alongside the things being said. Let your Intellect enter into the things happening and the things causing them.

7.31 Brighten yourself with simplicity and modesty, and with indifference toward the things lying between Virtue and Vice. Love the human race. Follow God. That one says that all things exist by convention, but in reality only the Atoms.[105] Yet it suffices to remember that all things are held by convention; and already that amounts to very few things.

7.32 Concerning death: either a scattering, if Atoms; or if a unity, then a quenching or a Transition.

7.33 Concerning pain: What is unbearable carries you off; what lingers is bearable. And the Mind preserves its own calm by withdrawing into itself, and the Ruling Faculty does not become worse. As for the parts injured by pain, let them, if they can, speak their opinion.[106]

7.34 Concerning glory: Look at their Minds; what sort they are, what things they flee, and what things they pursue. And just as sand-dunes heaped one upon another hide the previous ones, so in life the former things are very quickly covered over by those that come after.

7.35 "To the Mind, then, that possesses magnificence and contemplation of all time and all Substance, do you think human life seems to be anything great to such a one?" "Impossible," he said. "Then such a one will not consider death to be anything dreadful?" "Least of all."[107]

7.36 "It is Kingly to do good and be spoken of badly."[108]

7.37 "It is shameful that the face is obedient and shapes and composes itself as the Mind commands, but the Mind cannot shape and compose itself."

7.38 "One must not rage at things; for things do not care."

7.39 "May you give joy to the immortal Gods and to us."

7.40 "To harvest life as a ripe ear of grain. And for one to be, and the other not."[109]

7.41 "If the Gods have neglected me and my children: Even this has a Reason."[110]

7.42 "For with me is the Good and the Just."

7.43 "Do not join in their wailing, nor be agitated."

7.44 "For I would say a just word in reply to this: that you do not speak rightly, O man, if you think a man in whom there is even slight worth ought to calculate the risk of living or dying. Rather, one must look to this alone whenever he acts: whether he is doing what is just or what is unjust, and whether they are the works of a good man or of a bad one."

7.45 "For thus the matter truly stands, O men of Athens. Wherever a man places himself, thinking it the best, or is placed by a ruler, there, as it seems to me, he ought to stay and run the risk, calculating neither death nor anything else in preference to disgrace."

7.46 "But, my blessed one, look, is not the Noble and the Good something other than saving and being saved? For as for this, living for however long a time, the man who is truly a man must let it go and not love his life too much, but entrust these things to God. Believing the saying of the women, that no one can escape Fate, the next thing one must consider in what way he might live this time which he is about to live as best as possible."[111]

7.47 To survey the courses of the stars as if running around with them, and to think continuously on the Transformations of the Elements into one another. For the Impressions of these things cleanse away the filth of the life on the ground.

7.48 This is a fine saying of Plato: "That he who makes discourses about men should look upon earthly things as if from some place above: herds, armies, farms, weddings, divorces, births, deaths, the noise of law-courts, desert places, various nations of barbarians, feasts, lamentations, markets, the mixture of all things and the order composed of opposites."[112]

7.49 Observe the things that have happened long ago, the many Transformations of empires. You can foresee also the things that will be, for they will certainly be of like form, and it is not possible to step out of the rhythm of the things happening now. Therefore, to observe forty years of human life is equal to observing ten thousand. For what more will you see?

7.50 And the saying: "The things from earth return to earth; but the things of ethereal seed return again to the ethereal pole."

Or this: "A Dissolution of the interlacing of Atoms," and some such scattering of the impassive Elements.[113]

7.51 And: "With foods and drinks and magic charms turning aside the channel of death, so as not to die."

"But a wind blowing from the Gods one must endure with toil without lamentations."[114]

7.52 He is a better wrestler, but not more Social, nor more modest, nor more disciplined toward what happens, nor more gentle toward the oversights of neighbors.

7.53 Wherever it is possible to accomplish a work according to the Reason common to Gods and men, there is nothing terrible. For where it is possible to gain a benefit by means of activity that proceeds successfully and according to Constitution, there no harm should be suspected.

7.54 Everywhere and continuously it is in your power to be piously satisfied with the present circumstance, and to behave toward the people present with Justice, and to apply your Art to the present Impression, so that nothing unexamined slips in.

7.55 Do not look around at the Ruling Faculties of others; but look straight ahead directly to where Nature leads you: the Nature of the Whole leads you through the events in your life, and your own Nature through the things you must do. Everyone must do what follows from their Constitution.

Now, all other things have been constituted for the sake of the Rational beings, just as in everything else the inferior are for the sake of the better; but the Rational beings exist for the sake of one another. Therefore, the primary feature in the Constitution of man is the Social.

The second is resistance to bodily affections. For it is the property of Rational and Intellectual movement to limit itself and never to be defeated by either sensory movement or the movement of Impulse, for both of these are animal-like. But the Intellectual movement wishes to be first, and not to be mastered by those; and rightly so. For it is by nature made to use all those.

Third in the Rational Constitution is freedom from rashness and deception. Holding to these, then, let the Ruling Faculty proceed straight, and it possesses what is its own.

7.56 Consider yourself as one already dead, your life up to now complete. Now live what remains as a surplus, according to Nature.

7.57 Love only what has happened to you and is woven for you by Fate; for what is more fitting?

7.58 In every event, keep before your eyes those to whom the same things happened. They were grieved, were surprised, were complaining.

And now? Where are those people?

Nowhere.

Why then do you wish to be like them?

Why not leave those other changes to the changers and the changed, and you yourself be entirely concerned with how to use them?

For you will use them well, and they will be your Material; only pay attention and desire yourself to be good in everything you do. And remember both: that the Material on which you act is Indifferent, and that how you use it matters.

7.59 Dig within. Within is the fountain of the Good, and it is always able to bubble up, if you always dig.

7.60 The body too must be firmly set, and not scattered, neither in motion nor in posture. For just as the Mind provides a certain composure to the face, keeping it collected and well-formed, so one ought to demand the same of the whole body. But all these things must be maintained without affectation.

7.61 The Art of Living is more like wrestling than dancing, in this respect: that one stands ready and unshaken against things that fall upon one unforeseen.

7.62 Constantly consider who these people are whose testimony you wish to have, and what sort of Ruling Faculties they possess. For you will not blame those who stumble unwillingly, nor will you need their testimony, if you look into the sources of their opinions and Impulses.

7.63 "Every Psyche," he says,[115] "is deprived of the Truth unwillingly." And so too is it deprived of Justice, and Temperance, and Benevolence, and every such thing. It is most necessary to remember this constantly; for you will be gentler to all.

7.64 Regarding every pain, let this be ready: that it is not shameful, and it does not make the governing Mind worse. For it does not destroy it insofar as it is Rational or Social.

However, regarding most pains, let the saying of Epicurus help you: "Pain is neither unbearable nor eternal, if you remember its limits and do not add opinion to it."[116]

And remember this too: that many things which are the same as pain go unnoticed, though they are disagreeable, such as drowsiness, or heat, or loss of appetite. Whenever you are discontented with any of these, say to yourself: "I am yielding to pain."

7.65 Make sure that you do not feel toward the savages that which the savages feel toward other humans.

7.66 How do we know if Telauges[117] was not superior in character to Socrates? For it is not enough that Socrates died a more glorious death, that he argued more skillfully with the sophists, that he spent the night in the frost more patiently, that when ordered to arrest the Salaminian he seemed to resist more nobly, that he "swaggered in the streets"; about which one might especially pause to consider, if indeed it was true.[118]

But we must examine this: What sort of Psyche did Socrates have? Could he be content with being just toward men and pious toward the Gods? Was he neither annoyed without reason at Vice, nor enslaved to anyone's ignorance? Neither receiving any of the things apportioned from the Whole as foreign, nor enduring them as unbearable; nor surrendering the Intellect in Sympathy to the Passions of the paltry flesh?

7.67 Nature did not so blend the Mind with the bodily composition as to prevent it from setting its own boundaries and making its own things subject to itself. For it is very possible to be a 'divine man' and yet be recognized by no one. Always remember this. And remember also that a happy life requires very few things. And do not, just because you have despaired of becoming a logician or a physicist, give up on this account being free, modest, Social, and obedient to God.

7.68 Live out your life without constraint, in the utmost cheerfulness, even if all men shout whatever they want against you, and even if wild beasts tear apart the little limbs of this kneaded mass that has grown around you. For what prevents the Mind, in the midst of all this, from preserving itself in calmness, and in true Judgment concerning the surrounding circumstances, and in ready Use of whatever is placed before it? So that the Judgment may say to the Event: "This is what you are in Substance, even if you appear otherwise in Opinion." And the Use may say to the Object: "I was looking for you." For to me the Present is always Matter for Rational and Civic Virtue, and in summary, for the Art of humans or God. For everything that happens is proper to God or man, and is neither new nor difficult to manage, but familiar and workable.

7.69 The perfection of character is this: to live each day as if it were the last, and neither to be agitated, nor to go numb, nor to pretend.

7.70 The Gods, who are immortal, do not resent that for so vast an Eternity they must endure so vast a number of worthless people; and they even care for them in every way. But you, who are just about to die, you give up? And this when you are one of the worthless ones yourself!

7.71 It is ridiculous not to flee one's own Vice, which is possible, but to flee the Vice of others, which is impossible.

7.72 Whatever the Rational and Social Faculty finds to be neither Intellectual nor Social, it reasonably judges to be inferior to itself.

7.73 When you have done good and another has received good, why do you still seek, like the fools, a "third thing" besides these: the reputation of having done well, or a return?

7.74 No one grows tired of being helped. Benefit is an act according to Nature. So do not grow tired of being helped, while helping.

7.75 The Nature of the Whole set its Impulse toward the creation of a Cosmos. Now, either everything that happens follows by logical consequence, or else even the primary things, toward which the Ruling Faculty of the Cosmos directs its own Impulse, are irrational. Remembering this will make you calmer about many things.

8

Book 8

MARCUS ANTONINUS EMPEROR: To Himself. Book 8.

8.1 This too contributes to the casting away of empty glory: that you can no longer claim to have lived your whole life, or even from your youth, as a Philosopher. But to many others, and to you yourself, it is plain that you are far removed from Philosophy.

You have become disordered, so that acquiring a reputation as a Philosopher is no longer easy for you. Your position also opposes it. If, then, you have truly seen where the matter lies, dismiss the thought of how you shall seem to others, and be content if you live, even for the remainder of your life, however long that may be; as your Nature wills.

Understand then what she wills, and let nothing else distract you. For you have wandered through many things and nowhere found Flourishing. Not in syllogisms, not in wealth, not in fame, not in indulgence.

Nowhere.

Where is it, then?

In doing what Human Nature seeks. How then might you do this?

By holding Principles from which Impulses and Actions spring.

What Principles?

Those concerning Good and Evil: that there is nothing good for a man which does not make him Just, Temperate, Courageous, and free; and nothing is evil which does not produce the opposite of these.

8.2 With every action, ask yourself: how does this sit with me?

Might I regret it?

A little while and I am dead, and all things are gone from the midst.

What more do I seek, if the present work is of a Rational Animal, Social, and under the same law as God?

8.3 Alexander, and Gaius, or Pompey: what are they compared to Diogenes, and Heraclitus, or Socrates?[119]

For these saw the things, the Causes and the Matter, and their Ruling Faculties were self-sufficient. But as for the others; how many things they had to care for, and to how many were they enslaved!

8.4 Even if you burst, they will do the same things all the same.

8.5 First, do not be disturbed; for all things are according to the Nature of the Whole. And in a little while, you will be nobody and nowhere, just as Hadrian and Augustus are not now. Next, gaze intently at the thing and see it for what it is; and remembering that it is your duty to be a Good Man, and what Human Nature demands: do that without turning back. And speak as seems most Just to you, only with kindness, modesty, and without hypocrisy.

8.6 The Nature of the Whole has this work: to transfer what is here to there, to transform things, to lift them from here, and carry them there. All is Change: not so as to fear anything new.

All is familiar, and the apportionments are equal.

8.7 Every Nature is content with itself when it goes on its way well. A Rational Nature goes on its way well when it assents to nothing false or obscure in its Impressions, when it directs its Impulses only to Social acts, when it limits its Desires and Aversions to those things in our power, and

Why do you wonder? Even the Sun will say, "I have come into being for a certain work," and so the other Gods. And you, for what? For Pleasure?

See if the conception allows it.

8.20 Nature aimed at the end of each thing just as much as its beginning and its duration, like the one who throws a ball up.

What good is it to the little ball to go up? Or what evil to come down, or to fall? What good is it to the bubble while it holds together, or what evil when it bursts?

The same applies to a lamp.

8.21 Turn it inside out and see what sort of thing it is, and what it becomes when grown old, or sick, or whored. Short-lived are both the praiser and the praised, the rememberer and the remembered. And besides, [all this transpires only] in a corner of this region; and not even here do all agree; nor does anyone agree even with himself. And the whole earth is but a point.

8.22 Attend to the underlying subject, or to the Principle, or to the Action, or to the Meaning. You suffer this justly: you would rather become Good tomorrow than be Good today.

8.23 Am I doing something? I do it with reference to the good of mankind. Does something happen to me?

I accept it with reference to the Gods and to the source of all things, from which all that comes to be is spun together.

8.24 Consider what bathing appears to you: oil, sweat, filth, greasy water, all things disgusting: so is every part of life and every underlying thing.

8.25 Lucilla buried Verus, then Lucilla died.

Secunda buried Maximus, then Secunda died.

Epitynchanus buried Diotimus, then Epitynchanus died.

Antoninus buried Faustina, then Antoninus died.

Celer buried Hadrian, then Celer died.

So it is with all things.[120]

And where are those shrewd ones, or the prognosticators, or those puffed up with conceit?

Shrewd ones such as Charax, Demetrius the Platonist, Eudaemon, and others like them.[121] All ephemeral, long since dead. Some not remembered even for a little while, some passed into myths, some already faded even from the myths.

Remember these things, then: that your little composite must either be scattered, or your little Pneuma extinguished, or it must depart and be stationed elsewhere.

8.26 The joy of a human is to do what is proper to a human. And what is proper to a human is: Benevolence toward one's own kind, looking beyond the movements of the senses, discernment of plausible Impressions, and contemplation of the Nature of the Whole and all that happens in accordance with it.

8.27 We have three relationships: one to the Cause[122] that surrounds us, another to the Divine Cause from which all things happen to all, and a third to those who live with us.

8.28 Pain is either an evil to the body, then let the body say so, or to the Psyche. But it is in the power of the Psyche to preserve its own serenity and calm, and not to suppose that it is an evil. For every Judgment, Impulse, Desire, and Aversion is inside, and no evil ascends here.

8.29 Wipe away the Impressions, constantly telling yourself: It is now in my power that in this Psyche there be no depravity, no Desire, nor any disturbance at all; but seeing all things for what they are, I use each according to its worth. Remember this power which is according to Nature.

8.30 Speak both in the Senate and to anyone whatsoever with propriety, not pompously. Use sound speech.

8.31 The Court of Augustus:[123] his wife, his daughter, his descendants, his ancestors, his sister, Agrippa,[124] his kinsmen, his household, his friends, Areius, Maecenas, his physicians, his sacrificial priests: the death of the whole court. Then pass on to other cases, not the death of a single person, but of a whole family, like the Pompeys.[125]

And that inscription on tombs: 'The last of his own family line.'

Consider how zealously those before him strove to leave some successor, and yet by Necessity someone had to be the last. Here again, the death of a whole clan.

8.32 You must compose your life one action at a time, and be content if each one fulfills its own purpose as far as possible; and no one can prevent you from this.

"But some external obstacle will stand in the way."

None that can prevent you from acting justly, temperately, and reasonably.

"But perhaps some other actual activity will be hindered?"

Then, by welcoming the hindrance and by gracefully shifting your course to what is granted, you will immediately find another action as a substitute, one that fits into the composition we are discussing.

8.33 Receive without arrogance; but let go easily.

8.34 If you have ever seen a hand cut off, or a foot, or a head, lying somewhere apart from the rest of the body; that is what a man does to himself, as much as he can, when he does not will what happens and tears himself away, or when he does something unsocial. You have somehow cast yourself away from the union according to Nature, for you had naturally grown as a part; but now you have cut yourself off. Yet here is the elegant thing: it is in your power to unite yourself again. God has permitted this to no other part; once separated and cut through, to come together again. But consider the kindness with which he has honored man: for he made it within man's own power, in the first place, not to be torn away from the Whole, and even to one torn away, he has made it possible to return, grow together again, and recover his station as a part.

8.35 Just as the Nature of Rational beings has given nearly all the other Faculties to each Rational being, so too we have received this one from her as well. For just as she redirects whatever stands against and opposes her, converts it into Fate, and makes it a part of herself; so too the Rational Animal can make every obstacle Matter for itself, and employ it toward whatever end its Impulse may be directed.

8.36 Let not the Impression of your whole life confuse you. Do not mentally encompass how many painful things, and of what kind, are likely to befall you.

But for each of the present things, ask yourself: 'What in this task is unbearable and unendurable?'

For you will be ashamed to confess it. Then remind yourself that neither the future nor the past weighs upon you, but always the present. And this is minimized if you limit it alone, and convict your Mind if it cannot hold out against this bare thing.

8.37 Does Panthea or Pergamus[126] still sit by the tomb of Lucius?[127]

Or Chaurias[128] and Diotimus by the tomb of Hadrian?

Ridiculous.

And if they sat there, would the dead perceive it? And if they perceived it, would they be pleased? And if they were pleased, would the mourners be immortal? Was it not Fated that these too should first become old women and old men, and then die? What then would those emperors do afterward, when their mourners had died?

All these things are stench and gore in a bag.

8.38 If you can see sharply, look and judge, as he says, by the wisest standards.

8.39 I do not see, in the Constitution of the Rational Animal, a Virtue opposing Justice; but opposing Pleasure I see one: Self-Control.

8.40 If you remove your Opinion regarding what appears to give you pain, you yourself stand in the safest position.

"Who is 'yourself'?"

Reason.

"But I am not Reason."

Granted.

Let Reason, then, not hurt itself. But if something else in you is in a bad state, let it form its own Opinion about itself.

8.41 Hindrance to sensation is an evil to an animal nature. Hindrance to Impulse is likewise an evil to an animal nature. There is also something similarly obstructive and evil to the vegetative Constitution. So then, hindrance to Intellect is an evil to an Intellectual Nature. Apply all these to yourself.

Does Pain or Pleasure touch you?

Let the sense perception look to that.

Did an obstacle arise when you set out?

If you set out without Reservation, it is already an evil to you as a Rational being. But if you accept the common condition, you are not yet harmed nor hindered. Indeed, no one else is wont to hinder what is proper to the Intellect; for it is touched by neither fire nor steel, neither by tyrant nor by slander. When it has become a sphere, it remains round.[129]

8.42 I do not deserve to cause myself pain; for I never willingly caused pain to another.

8.43 Different things delight different people. My delight is to have my Ruling Faculty sound, not turning away from anyone or anything that happens to anyone, but looking on all things with benevolent eyes, accepting and using each according to its worth.

8.44 Look, give this time to yourself as a gift. Those who pursue posthumous fame more [than the present] do not consider that future people will be just like the people whom they find burdensome; and they too will be mortal. And what is it to you at all, if they should echo with such voices, or hold such and such an Opinion about you?

8.45 Lift me up and throw me wherever you will. For even there I shall keep my Daimon gracious; that is, content if it holds itself and acts in accordance with its own Constitution. Is this a worthy reason for my Psyche to be in a bad state, and to be worse than itself: abased, craving, fettered, and terrified? And what will you find worthy of that?

8.46 Nothing can happen to anyone which is not a human occurrence; nor to an ox which is not proper to an ox; nor to a vine which is not proper to a vine; nor to a stone which is not proper to a stone. If, then, what happens to each is both customary and natural, why should you be troubled? For the Common Nature brought nothing unbearable to you.

8.47 If you are pained on account of some external thing, it is not the thing that disturbs you, but your Judgment about it. And it is in your power to wipe this out immediately.

But if something in your own Disposition pains you, who prevents you from correcting your Doctrine?

And likewise, if you are pained because you are not doing some particular action which seems sound to you, why do you not rather act than be pained?

'But something stronger stands in the way.'

Then do not be pained; for the cause of the inaction is not from you.

'But it is not worth living if this is not done.'

Then depart from life graciously, in the manner of one who dies while acting, being at the same time kindly disposed toward those things that stand in the way.

8.48 Remember that the Ruling Faculty becomes unconquerable whenever, gathered into itself, it is content with itself, not doing anything which it does not will, even if it takes its stand unreasonably.[130] What then will it be when it judges concerning something with Reason and careful scrutiny? All the more so. Because of this, the Mind, free from Passions, is a citadel. For one has no stronger fortification into which he may flee and be hereafter impregnable. Anyone who has not seen this is ignorant; but one who has seen it and does not flee into it is unfortunate.

8.49 Say nothing more to yourself than what the primary Impressions report. It has been reported to you that so-and-so speaks ill of you. This has been reported. But that you have been harmed: this has not been reported. I see that the little child is sick. I see it. But that he is in danger: I do not see. Thus always abide by the first Impressions, and add nothing of your own from within, and nothing happens to you. Or rather, add as one who knows each thing that happens in the Cosmos.

8.50 Is the cucumber bitter?

Throw it away.

Are there brambles in the path?

Turn aside. It is enough.

Do not add: 'Why were such things made in the Cosmos?'

For you will be ridiculed by the student of Nature, just as you would be ridiculed by a carpenter or a shoemaker if you were offended because you saw shavings and scraps from the things being made lying in their workshop.

And yet they have somewhere to throw them; but the Nature of the Whole has nothing outside itself.

And yet the marvelous thing about this Art is that, having circumscribed itself, it transforms into itself everything within that seems corrupt, old, and useless; and makes again other new things from them; so that it neither needs Matter from outside, nor does it require a place to discharge the rotted things. It is content, therefore, with its own space, and its own Matter, and its own Art.

8.51 Do not drag along in your actions, nor be confused in your conversations, nor wander in your Impressions. Neither be wholly contracted in Psyche nor burst forth, nor be over-occupied in life. They kill, they butcher, they pursue with curses.

What then does this have to do with the Mind remaining pure, prudent, Temperate, and Just?

Just as if someone standing by a clear and sweet spring were to curse it, but it does not cease to bubble up fresh water. And even if he should throw in mud or dung, it will very quickly disperse them and wash them out, and in no way will be dyed by them.

How then will you possess a living spring and not a standing well?

By guarding yourself at every hour toward freedom: benevolently, simply, and with modesty.

8.52 He who does not know what the Cosmos is does not know where he is. He who does not know for what purpose he was born does not know who he is, nor what the Cosmos is. He who has failed to grasp one of these things could not even say for what he himself was born. What sort of person, then, does one appear to you who flees or pursues the praise of those who applaud: people who know neither where they are nor who they are?

8.53 Do you wish to be praised by a man who curses himself three times an hour? Do you wish to please a man who does not please himself? Does he please himself who repents of almost everything he does?

8.54 No longer merely breathe together with the air that surrounds you, but now think together with the Intellect that surrounds all things. For the Intellective Power is diffused everywhere and permeates all things for one who can draw it in, just as the Airy Power does for one who can breathe.

8.55 Vice generally does not harm the Cosmos at all. And particular Vice does not harm another. It is harmful only to that one person to whom it is granted to be released from it, as soon as he first wishes.

8.56 To my own Moral Will, the Moral Will of my neighbor is equally Indifferent, as is his bit of Pneuma and his bit of flesh. For even though we were born most of all for the sake of one another, yet our Ruling Faculties each have their own sovereignty. For otherwise, the Vice of my neighbor would be an evil to me; which God did not will, in order that my unhappiness might not depend on another.

8.57 The sunlight seems to be poured down, and indeed it is poured in all directions, yet it is not poured out. For this pouring is an extension. Thus its beams are extended. You may see what a 'beam' is, if you look at sunlight entering a dark room through a narrow opening. For it extends in a straight line and, as it were, presses against the solid body that meets it, blocking the air beyond. And there it stands, and does not slide off or fall. Such, then, should be the pouring and diffusion of the Mind: in no way a spilling out, but an extension. And against the obstacles that meet it, it should not be violent nor make a crashing impact, nor fall down, but stand still and illuminate what receives it. For that which does not transmit it will deprive itself of the radiance.

8.58 He who fears death fears either the loss of sensation or a different kind of sensation. But if you shall have no sensation, you will feel no harm; and if you acquire a different kind of sensation, you will be a different kind of living creature, and you will not cease to live.

8.59 Human beings exist for the sake of one another. Therefore: teach them, or bear with them.

8.60 An arrow travels one way, the Intellect another. Yet the Intellect, even when it exercises caution and circles around an inquiry, moves no less in a straight line toward its objective.

8.61 Enter into the Ruling Faculty of each person, and allow every other to enter into yours.

9

Book 9

9.1 He who acts unjustly acts impiously. For since the Nature of the Whole has constituted Rational Animals for the sake of one another (so as to benefit one another according to desert, but in no way to harm) he who transgresses her will clearly acts impiously against the most ancient of the Gods. And he who lies acts impiously against the same Goddess. For the Nature of the Whole is the Nature of things that exist; and things that exist stand in natural affinity with all things that are present. Further, this Goddess is named Truth, and is the first Cause of all things true.

Therefore, he who lies willingly acts impiously, insofar as he deceives and acts unjustly; and he who lies unwillingly acts impiously, insofar as he is discordant with the Nature of the Whole, and insofar as he creates disorder by fighting against the Nature of the Cosmos. For he fights against it who is carried by his own agency toward the contrary of Truth; for he had received from Nature certain endowments, which, having neglected, he is now unable to distinguish the false from the true. And indeed, he who pursues pleasures as goods and flees pains as evils acts impiously.

For it is a Necessity that such a man often blame the Common Nature as assigning things contrary to desert to the base and the excellent, since the base are often in enjoyment of pleasures and possess the things that produce them, while the excellent encounter pain and the things that produce pain. And further, he who fears pain will also at some time fear something that will happen in the Cosmos; and this is already impious. And he who pursues pleasure will not abstain from acting unjustly; and this is clearly impious.

But it is necessary that, regarding the things toward which the Common Nature is indifferent (for she would not have created both if she were not indifferent to both), those who wish to follow Nature be of the same mind and be indifferent toward these things. He, therefore, who is not himself indifferent to Pain and Pleasure, or Death and Life, or Glory and Obscurity (things which the Nature of the Whole uses indifferently) clearly acts impiously.

And by "uses indifferently," I mean that they happen indifferently in succession to the things that come to be, and to those things which come after them by a certain ancient Impulse of Providence, by which it set out from some first principle to create this ordering of things, having conceived certain Rational Principles of all that was to be, and having marked off the generative powers of such existences, Changes, and successions.

9.2 It would be a finer thing for a man to depart from life untouched by falsehood, hypocrisy, luxury, or pride. The next best course is to breathe one's last when surfeited with these things.

Or have you resolved to cling to Vice?

Has not experience yet taught you to flee this pestilence?

For a Decay of the Mind is a pestilence far more than any foulness or change in the air that surrounds us. The one is a plague to animals as animals; the other is a plague to men as men.

9.3 Do not despise death, but be well-disposed toward it, for it is one of the things that Nature wills. For as it is to be young, to grow old, to grow, to be in one's prime, to bring forth teeth and a beard and gray hairs, to beget, to carry in the womb, and to give birth (and all the other natural actions that the seasons of your life bring) so too is it to be dissolved. It is therefore the part of a man who has reasoned well to be neither dismissive, nor impatient, nor scornful of death, but to await it as one of Nature's processes. Just as you now await the time when the child will emerge from your wife's womb, so you should await the hour when your little Psyche will slip from this casing. But if you desire an ordinary remedy to touch the heart, what will make you face death most easily is to consider the things you are about to leave, and with what sorts of characters your Psyche will no longer be entangled. You ought not to take offense at them, but to care for them and bear with them gently. Yet remember that your departure is not from men who share your own principles. For this alone, if anything, could hold you back and bind you to life: if you were permitted to live with those who had embraced the same principles as yourself. But as it is, you see how great a weariness there is in the discord of life together, so that you might say: Come quickly, death, lest I too should forget myself.

9.4 He who does wrong does wrong to himself. He who acts unjustly harms himself, making himself evil.

9.5 He who does nothing often acts unjustly, not only he who does something.

9.6 These things suffice: the present Opinion cognitive, the present action communal, and the present disposition content with all that happens from an external Cause.

9.7 Wipe away Impressions. Halt Impulse. Extinguish Desire. Keep the Ruling Faculty within its own power.

9.8 Into irrational animals one Psyche has been divided, and into Rational beings one Intellectual Psyche has been distributed. Just as there is one earth for all things earthy, and we see by one light, and we breathe one air: all things that have sight and Psyche.

9.9 All things that share in something common hasten toward their own kind. The earthy is drawn to the earth, the watery flows together, and the airy does likewise, so that they require force to keep them apart.

Fire tends upward on account of the elemental fire, and it is so ready to be kindled along with all fire here that any matter that is a little dry is easily set ablaze, because there is less in it of what hinders ignition. So too, everything that partakes of the Common Intellectual Nature hastens toward its own kind, or even more so. For the more it excels other things, the more ready it is to mix with and be fused with its kin.

Thus, among irrational creatures, we find at once swarms, herds, the rearing of young, and a kind of love. For they already had Psyches, and the unifying principle is found intensified in the higher grade, such as was not present in plants or stones or wood. And among Rational Animals there are states and friendships, families and assemblies, and in war, treaties and truces.

Among beings still more excellent, a kind of unity exists even among things physically separate, as with the stars. Thus, the ascent to higher things could create Sympathy even among things that are apart. But see what happens now: only Intellectual beings have forgotten this mutual eagerness and inclination, and here alone the flowing together is not seen. Yet though they flee from it, they are still caught and held, for Nature prevails. You will see what I mean if you observe closely. For you will sooner find something earthy not touching another earthy thing than a man severed from man.

9.10 Man, God, and the Cosmos all bear fruit, each in its proper season. And if custom has restricted the word to the vine and the like, that is nothing. Reason, for its part, has fruit both common and particular, and from it are born other things of the same kind as Reason itself.

9.11 If you can, teach him better. If not, remember that for this purpose goodwill was given to you. The Gods themselves are well-disposed to such men, and in some matters (health, wealth, and glory) they even lend their aid, so gracious are they. You can be so too. Or tell me, who is stopping you?

9.12 Labor not as a wretch, nor as one who would be pitied or admired. Want one thing only: to be moved and to be restrained, as Civic Reason demands.

9.13 Today I escaped from all circumstance; or rather, I cast out all circumstance, for it was not outside, but within, in my own Judgments.

9.14 All these things are familiar by experience, ephemeral in time, and filthy in their Matter. All things now are as they were in the times of those we have buried.

9.15 Things stand outside our doors, by themselves, knowing nothing and declaring nothing about themselves. What, then, declares anything about them?
   The Ruling Faculty.

9.16 The evil and good of a Rational, Civic Animal lies not in being affected, but in activity; just as its Virtue and Vice lie not in being affected, but in activity.

9.17 For a stone thrown into the air, it is no evil to fall, nor any good to rise.

9.18 Penetrate within to their Ruling Faculties, and you will see what judges you fear, and what kind of judges they are of themselves.

9.19 All things are in a state of Transformation. You yourself are in perpetual Alteration and, in a sense, Decay. And so is the whole Cosmos.

9.20 Another's wrongdoing must be left with him.

9.21 The cessation of an activity, the cessation of an Impulse, the ceasing of a Judgment; and, as it were, a death: it is no evil. Turn now to the ages of your life; childhood, adolescence, young manhood, old age: each Transformation of these was a death. Was that so terrible? Turn then to the life you lived under your grandfather, then under your mother, then under your father. And as you find many other destructions,[131] Transformation, and endings, ask yourself: Was that so terrible?

So neither will be the ending, cessation, and Transformation of your whole life.

9.22 Hasten to your own Ruling Faculty, and to that of the Whole, and to your neighbor's. To your own, that you may make it just. To that of the Whole, that you may remember of what you are a part. To your neighbor's, that you may discern whether it was ignorance or intention, and at the same time consider that he is your kin.

9.23 Just as you yourself are a completing part of a Civic system, so let every act of yours be a completing part of Civic life. Whatever act of yours, therefore, does not have reference, either directly or remotely, to the Social end, tears your life apart and does not allow it to be one, and is seditious; just as in a populace, the man who, for his own part, stands apart from such concord.

9.24 Children's tantrums and games, and "You are a little Psyche carrying around a corpse", so that the Nekyia strikes us more vividly.[132]

9.25 Go to the quality of the Cause, and having marked it off from the Material element, contemplate it. Then determine the longest time that this peculiarly qualified thing can by its nature subsist.

9.26 You have endured countless troubles by not being content with your Ruling Faculty doing those things for which it was constituted. But enough.

9.27 When another blames you or hates you, or men utter such things about you, go to their little Psyches, enter within, and see what sort of people they are. You will see that you need not be torn apart so that they might hold any particular opinion of you. Yet you must be well-disposed toward them, for they are by nature friends. And the Gods, too, help them in all kinds of ways, by dreams and by oracles, to be sure, toward those things about which they concern themselves.

9.28 The cycles of the Cosmos are the same, up and down, from age to age. Either the Mind of the Whole initiates motion toward each individual thing (and if so, accept what it sets in motion) or it was set in motion once, and all the rest follows as a consequence. Or, in a certain manner, Atoms or indivisibles. In sum, if there is God,[133] all is well. If all is by chance, do not you too be governed by chance. Soon the earth will cover us all. Then the earth itself will be transformed, and that into which it transforms will be transformed again to infinity, and that again to infinity. If a man considers the waves of Transformation and Alteration, and their swiftness, he will despise everything mortal.

9.29 The Cause of the Whole is like a winter torrent: it sweeps everything along. How cheap are these little men who engage in public affairs and think they are acting like philosophers, dripping with snot and self-importance. Do what Nature now demands. Set about it, if it is given to you, and do not look around to see if anyone will know. Do not hope for Plato's Republic,[134] but be content if the smallest thing goes forward, and consider the result of this to be no small matter.

For who can change the opinions of men?

And without a change of opinion, what is there but the slavery of men who groan and pretend to obey?

Go on now and talk of Alexander, and Philip, and Demetrius of Phalerum.[135] I will follow them, if they saw what the Common Nature willed, and disciplined themselves. But if they were just tragic actors, no one has condemned me to imitate them. The work of philosophy is simple and modest. Do not lead me into pompous gravity.

9.30 Look down from above on countless herds, and countless ceremonies, and voyaging of every kind in storms and calms, and the differences among those being born, those living together, and those dying. Consider also the life lived by others long ago, and the life that will be lived after you, and the life now lived among barbarous nations. And how many do not even know your name, and how many will very soon forget it, and how many who perhaps praise you now will very soon blame you. And that neither memory nor fame nor anything else whatsoever is worth mentioning.

9.31 Tranquility regarding all that happens from the external Cause, and Justice in all that is done by the Cause originating from you: that is, Impulse and action finding their end in acting for the Common Good, as this is according to your Nature.

9.32 You can cut off many of the superfluous things that trouble you, for they lie entirely in your own Judgment. And you will at once make for yourself a vast space by grasping the whole Cosmos in your thought, and by contemplating your own lifetime,[136] and by thinking of the swift Transformation of each particular thing; how short the time from birth to Dissolution, and how vast the time before birth, just as the time after Dissolution is likewise boundless.

9.33 All that you see will very soon perish, and those who have witnessed them perishing will very soon perish themselves. And he who dies in extreme old age will come to the same state as he who dies prematurely.

9.34 What are their Ruling Faculties, and what do they strive for, and on what grounds do they love and honor?

Imagine you see their naked little Psyches. When they think they harm us with their blame, or help us with their praise, what a conceit!

9.35 Loss is nothing else but Transformation. And in this the Nature of the Whole delights, by which all things are well done.

From Eternity all things have been of a similar form, and so they will be to infinity. What then do you say?

That all things have been and always will be evil, and that among so many Gods no power has ever been found to correct them, but the Cosmos is condemned to be afflicted with unending evils?

9.36 The rottenness of the Matter underlying each thing: water, dust, little bones, stench.

And again, marble is but a callus of the earth, gold and silver its sediments; our clothes are but hair, and the purple dye is blood. All other things are of the same kind. And the little Pneuma[137] too is another such thing, transforming from this to that.

9.37 Enough of this wretched life, of murmuring, and of apish tricks. Why are you disturbed? What is new in this? What throws you out of your senses? The Cause? Look at it. Matter? Look at it. Besides these, there is nothing. But toward the Gods, become at last simpler and better. It is the same whether you observe these things for a year or for three.[138]

9.38 If he has sinned, the evil lies with him. But perhaps he has not sinned.

9.39 Either all things from one intelligent source happen together as in one body, and the part ought not to blame what happens for the sake of the Whole: or Atoms, and nothing else but mixture and scattering.

Why then are you disturbed?

Do you say to your Ruling Faculty: "Are you dead? Are you corrupted? Have you become a beast? Do you act? Do you herd? Do you graze?"

9.40 Either the Gods have no power, or they have power.

If they have no power, why do you pray?

But if they have power, why do you not rather pray for them to give you the ability neither to fear any of these things, nor to desire any of them, nor to be grieved by any of them, rather than praying for their presence or absence?

For surely, if they can assist men at all, they can assist them in this.

But perhaps you will say, "The Gods have placed these things in my own power."

Then is it not better to use what is in your power with freedom, than to be anxiously concerned about what is not in your power with servility and abasement?

And who told you that the Gods do not assist us even in things that are in our power?

Begin, then, to pray for these things, and you will see.

One man prays: "How might I lie with that woman!"

You: "How might I not desire to lie with her!"

Another: "How might I be rid of that man!"

You: "How might I not need to be rid of him!"

Another: "How might I not lose my little child!"

You: "How might I not fear to lose him!"

Turn your prayers entirely in this direction, and observe what happens.

9.41 Epicurus says that in his illness, his conversations were not about the sufferings of his poor body, nor did he talk of such things to those who visited him. Rather, he continued to discourse on the principal doctrines of natural philosophy. He said his Mind was intent on this: how, though it partakes in such agitations of the poor flesh, it might remain undisturbed and guard its own proper good. Nor did he allow the physicians to puff themselves up as if accomplishing something, but his life went on well and happily.

What he did in sickness, you should do in sickness or in any other circumstance. For it is common to every school of philosophy not to abandon philosophy in whatever circumstances befall, nor to engage in idle talk with the layman ignorant of natural philosophy. One must attend only to the business at hand, and to the instrument by which it is accomplished.[139]

9.42 When you are offended by someone's shamelessness, ask yourself at once: Can it be that there are no shameless people in the Cosmos?

It cannot.

Do not, then, ask for the impossible. For this man is one of those shameless people who must exist in the Cosmos. Let the same thought be ready for the thief, the faithless man, and every other kind of wrongdoer. For by remembering that it is impossible for this kind of man not to exist, you will be more charitable toward each one.

It is also useful to consider at once what Virtue has Nature given man to oppose that particular fault. For she has given gentleness as an antidote to the ungrateful, and another power against another kind of man. And in general, you have the power to re-instruct one who has gone astray, for every man who sins is missing his proper mark and has gone astray.

And finally, what harm have you suffered?

For you will find that none of those by whom you are angered has done anything by which your Mind could be made worse; and it is in the Mind alone that evil and harm have their existence.

And what is so evil or strange if an uneducated man acts like an uneducated man?

See that you do not rather blame yourself, for not having expected that he would commit this fault. For Reason gave you the faculties to surmise that it was likely he would sin in this way, and yet, having forgotten this, you are amazed that he has done so.

But most of all, when you blame a man for being faithless or ungrateful, turn to yourself. For the fault is undoubtedly your own, if you trusted that a man of that character would keep his promise; or if, when you conferred a benefit, you did not confer it absolutely, nor in such a way as to receive the full fruit from your action itself.

For what more do you want when you have done a man a kindness?

Is it not enough that you have acted in accordance with your Nature?

Do you seek a reward for it?

It is as if the eye were to demand a reward for seeing, or the feet for walking. For just as these parts were made for a particular purpose, and by acting according to their own Constitution they attain their proper end, so a man, born for beneficence, when he has done some beneficent act or anything else that contributes to the Common Good, has done what he was constituted for, and has what is his own.

10

Book 10

MARCUS ANTONINUS EMPEROR: To Himself. Book 10.

10.1 Will you ever, O my Psyche, be good, and simple, and one, and naked, more visible than the Body that surrounds you?

Will you ever taste the disposition that loves and wants nothing?[140]

Will you ever be full and without want, desiring nothing, yearning for nothing, neither animate nor inanimate: for the enjoyment of pleasures?

Nor needing time in which to enjoy them longer?

Nor needing a specific place, or country, or favorable climate?

Nor the harmony of men?

But will you be content with your present condition, and pleased with all that you have right now?

And will you convince yourself that everything is yours, and everything is well with you, and comes from the Gods?

And that all will be well, whatever is dear to them, and whatever they shall give for the preservation of the Perfect Living Being; the Good and Just and Beautiful, which generates and holds together and contains and embraces all things that are dissolving into the Generation of other similar things?

Will you ever be such that you can live as a fellow citizen with Gods and men, so as neither to find fault with them nor be condemned by them?

10.2 Watch what your Nature requires, so far as you are governed by Nature alone. Then do it and accept it: provided your nature as a living creature is not made worse by it.

Next, watch what your nature as a living creature requires, and accept all of it: provided your nature as a Rational Animal is not made worse by it.

Now, the Rational is immediately also the Social.

Use these rules, then, and trouble yourself about nothing else.

10.3 Everything that happens either happens in a way that you are by nature fitted to bear, or in a way that you are not. If then something happens to you in a way you are naturally fitted to bear, do not be vexed: bear it as you are by nature fitted to bear it. But if it happens in a way you are not naturally fitted to bear, do not be vexed, for it will perish after consuming you. Remember, however: you are by nature fitted to bear everything concerning which it lies within your own Judgment to render it bearable and endurable, according to the Impression that it is beneficial, or a duty for yourself, to do so.

10.4 If someone errs, teach him gently and point out what is being overlooked. But if you cannot, blame yourself, or not even yourself.

10.5 Whatever happens to you was being prepared for you from Eternity, and the interweaving of Causes spun together from everlasting both your own Substance and the occurrence of this event.

10.6 Whether Atoms or Nature: first, let it be established that I am a part of the Whole governed by Nature; next, that I have a certain natural kinship with the parts of the same kind. For remembering these things (insofar as I am a part) I will be displeased with nothing assigned to me from the Whole. For nothing is harmful to the part which is advantageous to the Whole. For the Whole contains nothing that is not advantageous to itself; all natures having this in common, but the Nature of the Cosmos having this additionally: that it is not compelled by any external Cause to generate anything harmful to itself.

By remembering, therefore, that I am a part of such a Whole, I will be content with everything that happens. And insofar as I have a kinship with the parts of the same kind, I will do nothing unsocial. Rather, I will aim at those of the same kind, and turn all my Impulse toward the common advantage, and divert it from the opposite. With these things proceeding thus, life must necessarily flow well; just as you would conceive the life of a citizen to flow well who proceeds through actions beneficial to his fellow citizens, and embraces whatever the City assigns.

10.7 For the parts of the Whole (as many as are by nature contained within the Cosmos) it is necessary to perish. Let this be understood as signifying "to be altered." But if this were both an evil by nature and a necessity for them, the Whole would not fare well, with its parts tending toward alienation[141] and variously constructed for perishing.

Did Nature herself, then, undertake to harm her own parts, making them liable to evil and by necessity falling into evil? Or did such things escape her notice? Both are unbelievable.

But if someone, setting aside Nature, should explain these things simply according to natural Constitution, even so it is ridiculous to say on the one hand that the parts of the Whole are naturally constituted to transform, and on the other hand to be amazed or annoyed as if something contrary to Nature were happening, especially when the Dissolution occurs into those very Elements from which each thing is composed.

For it is either a scattering of Elements from which it was compounded, or a turning of the solid into the earthy and of the Pneumatic into the airy; so that these too are taken back into the Reason of the Whole, whether it is periodically consumed by fire or renewed by eternal alternations.

And as for the solid and the Pneumatic, do not imagine these to be the same as those from your original birth. For all this received its influx only yesterday or the day before from foods and the air being drawn in. Therefore, it is this which transforms, not that which your mother bore.

But suppose that original matter binds you very closely to the peculiarly qualified individual: even so, I think this is nothing against what is now being said.

10.8 Having given yourself these names (Good, Modest, True, Prudent, Concordant, High-minded) take care that you are never renamed; and if you lose these names, return to them quickly.

And remember that "Prudent" was intended to signify to you a discriminating attention to each particular thing, and freedom from negligence. "Concordant" signifies the voluntary acceptance of what is assigned by Common Nature. And "High-minded" signifies the elevation of the Thinking Part above the smooth or rough motions of the flesh, and above petty glory, and death, and all such things.

If, therefore, you maintain yourself in these names, without craving to be called by these names by others, you will be a different person, and you will enter into a different life. For to continue being such as you have been until now, and to be torn apart and defiled in such a life, is the mark of a man utterly senseless and clinging to life; like the half-devoured beast-fighters[142] who, covered with wounds and gore, nevertheless beg to be kept until the morrow, only to be thrown again in that state to the same claws and bites.[143]

Embark, then, into these few names. And if you are able to abide in them, abide as one who has relocated to some Islands of the Blessed.[144] But if you perceive that you are falling away and cannot maintain your hold, go courageously into some corner where you can regain control; or even depart from life altogether, not in anger, but simply, freely, and modestly, having done at least this one thing in life: to have departed from it thus.

However, for the remembrance of these names, it will greatly help you to remember the Gods, and that they do not wish to be flattered, but wish all Rational beings to become like themselves; and that a fig tree should do the work of a fig tree, a dog the work of a dog, a bee the work of a bee, and a man the work of a man.

10.9 Farce, War, Panic, Sloth, and Slavery will wipe out those sacred principles of yours every day; principles you form Impressions of and let slip by without study of Nature. You must look at everything and act in such a way that the practical is accomplished, the theoretical is exercised, and the self-reliant confidence that comes from Knowledge of each thing is preserved: unobtrusive, yet not concealed.

When will you enjoy simplicity? When dignity? When clear Knowledge of each thing: what it is in Substance, what place it holds in the Cosmos, how long it is naturally constituted to exist, from what it is compounded, to whom it can belong, and who has the power to give it and take it away?

10.10 A little spider, having caught a fly, thinks itself grand. Another man is proud of a little hare; another of a tiny anchovy in his net; another of little pigs; another of bears; another of Sarmatians.[145] If you examine their principles, are these not brigands?

10.11 Acquire a contemplative method for seeing how all things transform into one another. Attend to this continually and train yourself in this subject. For nothing is so conducive to Magnanimity.

Such a person has stripped off the Body; and knowing that very soon he must leave all this behind and depart from humankind, he dedicates his whole self to Justice in his own actions and to the Nature of the Whole in everything else that happens.

What anyone will say, think, or do against him he does not even take into Mind, being content with these two things alone: to act justly in what is presently being done, and to love the lot now being assigned to him. All occupations and anxious pursuits he has let go. He wants nothing else but to travel the straight path according to Law, and by traveling it, to follow God.

10.12 What need is there for conjecture, when it is possible to examine what must be done? And if you see it clearly, proceed this way with good will, without turning back. But if you do not see it, suspend judgment and use the best counselors. But if other things stand in the way, proceed according to your present opportunities with calculation, holding fast to what appears Just. For to attain this is best, since indeed failure consists in falling away from it. He who follows Reason in all things is at once unhurried and yet nimble, cheerful and yet composed.

10.13 Ask yourself as soon as you wake from sleep: "Will it make any difference to you if what is Just and Noble is done by another?"

It will not make a difference.

Have you forgotten what sort of people these are, those who prance and snort over their praises and blames of others, what they are like in bed, what they are like at table?

What sort of things they do?

What sort of things they flee?

What sort of things they pursue, what they steal, what they plunder?

Not with hands and feet, but with their most precious part; which becomes, whenever it wills: Faith, Modesty, Truth, Law, and a Good Daimon.

10.14 To Nature, who gives all things and takes them back, the educated and reverent person says: "Give what you wish; take back what you wish."

He says this not defiantly, but only in obedience and with goodwill toward her.

10.15 Little remains of this life. Live as on a mountain. For it makes no difference whether there or here, if one lives everywhere as in a City: the Cosmos. Let men see, let them examine a true human being living according to Nature. If they cannot bear him, let them kill him. For that is better than to live thus.

10.16 No longer talk all about what a good man ought to be, but be one.

10.17 Continuously form an Impression of the whole of Eternity and the whole of Substance, and recognize that all particular things are, in relation to Substance, a millet seed; and in relation to Time, the turning of a drill.

10.18 Directing attention to each underlying thing, conceive of it as already dissolving, in Transformation, and as it were becoming Decay or dispersal;

or according to how each thing is naturally constituted, as it were, to die.

10.19 What are they like when eating, sleeping, fucking, shitting, and everything else?

And then what are they like when lording it over others and puffing themselves up with pride, or raging and rebuking from a position of superiority?

A short while ago they were slaves to how many [Passions], and for what petty things!

10.20 It is beneficial to each, whatever the Nature of the Whole brings to each. And it is beneficial precisely at that time when Nature brings it.

10.21 "Earth loves the rain; and the sacred Aether loves."[146]

And the Cosmos loves to create whatever is about to happen.

I say, therefore, to the Cosmos: "I share in your love."

Is this not also what is meant by the expression: "This loves to happen?"

10.22 Either you remain here and have grown used to it; or you leave, and this is your own will; or you die, and your service is finished. Apart from these three, there is nothing else. So take heart.

10.23 Let it always be clear to you that the countryside is of the same character as here, and how all things here are the same as those on a mountain peak, or by the seashore, or wherever you wish. For you will find exactly what Plato [describes]: "enclosing a fold on a mountain," he says, "and milking his bleating flock."[147]

10.24 What is my Ruling Faculty to me?

And what sort of thing am I making it right now?

And to what purpose am I now using it?

Is it empty of Intellect?

Is it loosed and torn away from Community?

Is it melted together and mixed with the wretched flesh, so as to be turned along with it?

10.25 He who flees his master is a fugitive slave.[148] The Law is master; therefore, he who transgresses the Law is a fugitive slave.

But also he who grieves, or is angry, or fears does not wish something to have happened (or to be happening, or to be about to happen) from among the things ordained by the one who governs all things. This one is Law, distributing to each what falls to him. Therefore, he who fears, or grieves, or is angry is a fugitive slave.

10.26 Having discharged semen into a womb, he withdrew.[149] Then another Cause takes over, and works and completes an infant.

What a thing from such a source!

Again: food was released through the throat, and then another Cause, taking over, produces sensation and Impulse and, in sum, life and strength, and other things: how many and of what kinds!

Contemplate these things that are produced in such secrecy, and see the power, just as we see the power that makes things sink and rise,[150] not with our eyes, but no less clearly.

10.27 Constantly consider how all things are of the same kind as those that now occur, and also occurred before; and consider that they will occur again. Place before your eyes entire dramas and stagings of the same type, which you know from your own experience or from older history: the whole court of Hadrian, the whole court of Antoninus, the whole court of Philip, of Alexander, of Croesus. For all those were the same, only through different actors.[151]

10.28 Imagine that everyone who grieves or is discontented at anything is like a piglet being sacrificed, kicking and squealing. Like this too is the man who lies alone on his little bed, silently lamenting our bondage. Consider that to the Rational Animal alone is it granted to follow willingly what happens;

for merely to follow is a necessity for all.

10.29 In each specific thing you do, stop and ask yourself: "Is death a dreadful thing because it deprives me of *this*?"

10.30 When you take offense at someone's error, immediately shift and consider: what similar error do you commit?

For example, judging money to be Good, or Pleasure, or petty reputation, and such like. By swiftly applying this to yourself, you will quickly forget your Anger, as it simultaneously occurs to you that the man is compelled: for what else can he do?

Or, if you are able, remove the compulsion from him.

10.31 When you see Satyron, imagine Socraticus[152] or Eutyches or Hymen. And when you see Euphrates, imagine Eutychion or Silvanus. And when you see Alciphron, imagine Tropaeophorus. And when you see Xenophon, imagine Crito or Severus. And looking at yourself, imagine one of the Caesars. And regarding each person, make the analogy.[153]

Then let the thought strike you: "Where are they now?"

Nowhere, or anywhere.

For in this way you will constantly view human affairs as smoke and nothingness, especially if you recall that what has once transformed will no longer exist in infinite time.

Why then are you straining?

Is it not enough for you to pass this brief time in a decent manner?

What sort of material and subject matter are you fleeing?

For what are all these things other than exercises for Reason that has viewed life precisely and according to natural philosophy?

Stay with them, then, until you have assimilated even these things to yourself, just as a strong stomach assimilates all food, or as a bright fire turns whatever you throw into it into flame and light.

10.32 Let no one be able to say of you truthfully that you are not simple or not good. Let him be a liar, whoever thinks any of this about you. This is entirely up to you. For who prevents you from being good and simple?

Only resolve not to live any longer if you will not be such a man; for Reason does not choose one who is not.

10.33 Upon this present matter, what is the soundest thing that can be done or said?

For whatever that may be, it is in your power to do or say it; do not make the excuse that you are hindered.

You will never cease your lamentations until you undergo this condition: that as luxury is to pleasure-seekers, so to you is acting in accordance with the Constitution of a human being upon the matter presented to you. For you ought to regard as enjoyment everything that you are able to do in accordance with your own Nature; and this is allowed everywhere.

It is not allowed to a cylinder to move everywhere by its own motion, nor to water, nor to fire, nor to the other things governed by Nature or an irrational Psyche; for there are many things that hold them back and stop them. But Intellect and Reason are able to proceed through every opposing thing, as their nature and their will incline them.

Place before your eyes this ease with which Reason is carried through all things, as fire goes up, as a stone comes down, as a cylinder rolls down a slope, and seek nothing further. For all remaining obstacles either belong to the poor little body (which is a corpse), or else, without the yielding of Opinion and the surrender of Reason itself, they neither crush nor do any harm whatsoever. Otherwise, he who suffered them would himself immediately become bad. In all other creations, if some harm happens to them, the thing itself becomes worse; but here, the man becomes (if one may say so) better and more praiseworthy by making right use of what befalls him.

In general, remember that nothing harms the Citizen by nature which does not harm the City; and nothing harms the City which does not harm the Law. But none of these so-called misfortunes harms the Law; therefore, they harm neither the City nor the Citizen.

10.34 For one who has been bitten by true principles, even the briefest and most ordinary saying suffices as a reminder of freedom from Distress and Fear. For example:

"Leaves: some the wind pours down to the ground; such is the generation of men."[154]

Little leaves, too, are your little children. Little leaves, too, are those who shout with seeming credibility and bless you, or, from the opposite side, curse you, or quietly blame and sneer. Little leaves, likewise, are those who will inherit your posthumous fame. For all these things "spring up in the season of spring," then the wind casts them down, and then the woodland produces others in their place.

Briefness of life is common to all things. Yet you flee and pursue everything as if it were to be eternal. A little while, and you will close your eyes; and the one who has already carried you out for burial, another will mourn him.

10.35 A healthy eye ought to look at everything visible, and not say, "I want only green things"; for this is the mark of a diseased eye. And healthy hearing and smell ought to be ready for everything audible or smellable. And a healthy stomach should be disposed the same way toward all food, as a mill is toward all it was made to grind.

So, too, a healthy Mind ought to be prepared for everything that happens. But the Mind that says, "Let my little children be safe," or "Let everyone praise whatever I do," is an eye looking for green things, or teeth looking for something soft.

10.36 There is no one so fortunate[155] that, when he is dying, there will not be some standing by who welcome the sadness coming to him. He was a serious and wise man, let us say. But will there not be someone at the end who says to himself, "At last we can breathe freely again, without this schoolmaster! He was not harsh to any of us, but I always felt that he was silently condemning us." This is for a good man.

But for us, how many other reasons are there for which many would be glad to be rid of us? Think of this when you are dying, and you will depart more easily if you reason: "I am leaving a life from which my very partners, for whom I struggled so much, prayed, and cared, wish me to go, hoping perhaps for some relief from it." Why then should one strive to stay longer?

Yet do not leave them with less good will on this account, but preserve your own character: friendly, benevolent, and gracious. Do not leave as if being torn away; but rather, as when a man dies an easy death and the Psyche is effortlessly released from the body, so should be your departure from these men. For Nature bound you to them and united you. But now she dissolves the bond. I am dissolved, then, not dragged apart, but not resisting. For this, too, is one of the things in accord with Nature.

10.37 Accustom yourself, in everything that is done by another, to ask yourself as far as possible: "To what does this reference lead?"

But begin with yourself, and examine yourself first.

10.38 Remember that the thing which pulls the strings is the power hidden within: that is the persuasion, that is the life, that, one might say, is the man.

Never confuse it in your imagination with the vessel that contains it and these limbs that are molded around it. For they are like tools (an adze, for instance) differing only in that they are attached naturally. For without the cause that moves and checks them, these parts are of no more use than the shuttle to the weaver, the pen to the writer, or the whip to the charioteer.

11

Book 11

MARCUS ANTONINUS EMPEROR: To Himself. Book 11.

11.1 These are the properties of the Rational Psyche: It sees itself, it shapes itself, it makes itself what it chooses to be, and it reaps its own fruit; whereas the fruit of plants and the issue of animals are gathered by others. It attains its own end, wherever life's end may find it. Unlike in a dance, a play, or a similar performance, where any interruption leaves the whole action incomplete, the Rational Psyche, in any part of its action and wherever it is overtaken, makes what it has set for itself complete and self-sufficient, so that it can say, "I have what is my own."

Furthermore, it ranges over the whole Cosmos, the Void that surrounds it, and its shape. It extends into the infinity of time, and it grasps the periodic rebirth of all things, contemplating that those who come after us will see nothing new, nor did our ancestors see anything more than we have. In a way, a man of forty, if he has any understanding at all, has seen all that has been and all that will be, for it is all of one kind.

These too are properties of the Rational Psyche: love of one's neighbor, Truth, and self-respect, and to honor nothing more than itself. This is also a property of the universal Law, so that there is no difference between right Reason and the Reason of Justice itself.

11.2 You will despise a pleasant song, a dance, or the pancratium[156] if you break down a melodious voice into its individual notes and ask yourself of each one, "Am I mastered by this?"

You will shrink back.

Do the same with dancing, for each movement and posture.

Do the same with the pancratium.

In general, then, with respect to all things other than Virtue and its works, remember to go to their constituent parts and, by this analysis, you will come to despise them. Apply this method to your whole life.

11.3 What kind of Psyche is the one that is prepared, if it should now be necessary to be released from the body: whether to be extinguished, scattered, or to endure! But this readiness must come from its own judgment, not from mere obstinacy, as with the Christians,[157] but rationally and with dignity, and in a way that can persuade another, without theatrical display.

11.4 I have done something for the Common Good; I have therefore received my reward. Let this thought be always at hand, and never cease.

11.5 What is your art?

To be good.

And how is this accomplished well except through principles, some concerning the Nature of the Whole, others concerning the particular Constitution of man?

11.6 First, Tragedies were introduced to remind us of events that happen, and that it is in their nature to happen so, and that if you are delighted by them on the stage, you should not be distressed by them on the greater stage.

For you see that these things must be accomplished thus, and that even those who cry out "Alas, Cithaeron!" bear them.[158]

And the playwrights say some useful things, such as this in particular: "If I and my children have been neglected by the Gods, this too has its reason."[159]

And again: "For one must not rage against circumstances."[160]

And: "To reap life like a ripe ear of grain," and other things of that kind.[161]

After Tragedy came Old Comedy, with its pedagogical frankness, usefully reminding us of freedom from conceit through its very plain-spokenness. Diogenes too employed these methods for the same purpose. After these, consider what Middle Comedy is, and finally for what purpose New Comedy has been adopted: how it gradually slipped into mere artistry derived from imitation. It is not unknown that these too contain some useful sayings, but toward what aim has the whole undertaking of such poetry and drama-making looked?[162]

11.7 How clearly it strikes one that no other course of life is so suited to the practice of philosophy as this one you are now in.

11.8 A branch cut from an adjacent branch is necessarily cut from the whole tree. So too a man severed from another man has fallen away from the whole Community. A branch is cut off by another, but a man separates himself from his neighbor through his own hatred and aversion, not realizing that he has thereby cut himself off from the whole Social body.

Yet we have this gift from Zeus, who founded this Community: we are able to grow together again with the one nearby and once more become completers of the Whole. But if this separation happens repeatedly, it makes the reunion and restoration of the severed part difficult. And in general, the branch that grew with the tree from the start and remained sharing its breath is not the same as the one that is grafted back on after being cut, as the gardeners say: "To share the same bush, but not the same doctrine."

11.9 Just as those who oppose you as you advance according to right Reason will not be able to turn you from sound action, so too let them not deflect you from your goodwill toward them. Guard yourself equally in both: not only in sound judgment and action, but also in gentleness toward those who try to hinder you or are otherwise displeased. For it is a sign of weakness to be angry with them, just as it is to abandon your course and surrender in fear. For both are equally deserters: the man who cowers, and the man who is alienated from one who is by Nature kin and friend.

11.10 No Nature is inferior to art, for the arts imitate natures. If this is so, then the Nature that is most perfect and all-encompassing would not fall short of artistic ingenuity. Moreover, all arts make the inferior for the sake of the superior; so too does the Common Nature. And from this, Justice has its origin, and from it the other Virtues have their foundation. For Justice cannot be preserved if we are distracted by indifferent things, or if we are easily deceived, rash, and changeable.

11.11 The things whose pursuit and avoidance disturb you do not come to you; rather, in a certain way, you yourself rush toward them. Let your judgment concerning them be still, and they too will remain motionless, and you will not be seen either pursuing or avoiding.

11.12 The Psyche is a sphere, self-formed, when it neither reaches out toward anything, nor contracts inward, nor is scattered, nor subsides, but shines with the light by which it sees the truth of all things and the truth within itself.

11.13 Will someone despise me?

Let him see to it. I will see to it that I am not found doing or saying anything that deserves contempt.

Will someone hate me?

Let him see to it. As for me, I will be mild and benevolent to all, and ready to show even this very man what he overlooks, not in a scolding way, nor to display my patience, but genuinely and with good will, like that famous Phocion,[163] if indeed he was not pretending.

For this is how a man's inner self should be, and he should be seen by the Gods as one who is not resentfully disposed toward anything, nor taking things hard.

For what harm is it to you, if you are now doing what is proper to your own Nature, and you accept what is now opportune for the Nature of the

Whole; you, a man straining toward bringing about the Common Good by whatever means?

11.14 They despise one another, yet they flatter one another; they seek to get above one another, yet they bow down to one another.

11.15 How rotten and insincere is the man who says: "I have decided to be straightforward with you." What are you doing, man? There is no need for such a preface; the fact will show itself. It should be written on your forehead. Your voice should sound it at once; it should show in your eyes, just as the beloved knows everything at a glance from the look of his lovers.

The good and simple man should be like one who smells of goat:[164] the moment someone comes near, he perceives it, whether he wants to or not. But the pretense of simplicity is a dagger. Nothing is more shameful than a predatory friendship. Avoid this above all. The good, simple, and benevolent man has these qualities in his eyes, and they cannot be hidden.

11.16 To live most excellently: this power resides in the Psyche, if it is indifferent to Indifferent things. It will be indifferent if it examines each of them both separately and as a whole, remembering that none of them imposes upon us an Opinion about itself, nor comes to us. They remain still; it is we who generate judgments about them and, as it were, inscribe them upon ourselves; though we have the power not to inscribe them, or to wipe them away at once if they have crept in unawares. Such Attention is only for a short time, and presently life will have ceased.

Yet what is difficult about these things being otherwise?

If they are according to Nature, rejoice in them and let them be easy for you. If they are contrary to Nature, seek what accords with your own Nature and strive for that, even if it brings no glory. For everyone is forgiven for seeking their own good.

11.17 Consider whence each thing has come, from what underlying materials each arises, into what it transforms, what it will be like having transformed, and that it will suffer no evil.

11.18 First, what is my relationship to others?

We were born for the sake of one another. And from another point of view, I was born to be their leader, like a ram for the flock or a bull for the herd. Begin from the first principles: if all is not Atoms, it is Nature that governs the Whole. If so, then the lower exist for the sake of the higher, and the higher for the sake of one another.

Second, what are they like at table, in bed, and elsewhere? Above all, what principles are they slaves to, and with what arrogance do they perform these very acts?

Third, if they do right, you must not be angry. But if they do wrong, it is clear they do so unwillingly and in ignorance. For just as every Psyche is unwillingly deprived of the truth, so it is unwillingly deprived of the power to treat each person as he deserves. And so men are pained to be called unjust, ungrateful, greedy, and in short, wrongdoers to their neighbors.

Fourth, you also are guilty of many faults and are just like them. And if you do abstain from some wrongs, you still have the disposition to commit them, even if it is from cowardice, or concern for your reputation, or some other base motive that you hold back.

Fifth, you cannot even be sure they are doing wrong, for many things are done with a specific purpose in mind. In general, one must learn a great deal before one can pronounce with certainty on another's actions.

Sixth, when you greatly suffer, remember that human life is short, and in a little while we are all laid out for burial.

Seventh, it is not their actions that disturb us; for those are based in their own Ruling Faculties, but our own Opinions of them. Remove it, then, and resolve to dismiss your judgment that it is a terrible thing, and your Anger is gone. How to remove it? By reflecting that it does you no dishonor. For if what is dishonorable is not the only evil, you too must necessarily do many wrong things and become a robber and a scoundrel.

Eighth, how much more harmful are the Anger and Distress that their actions produce in us than the actions themselves that make us angry and grieve.

Ninth, kindness is invincible, if it is genuine and not a smirk or a pretense. For what can the most violent man do to you if you remain consistently kind to him, and if the opportunity arises, you gently admonish him and calmly correct his error at the very moment he is trying to harm you?

"No, my child. We were born for other things. I will not be harmed, but you are harming yourself, my child."

And show him tactfully and in general terms that this is so, and that not even bees do this, nor any of the other animals that are Social by nature. But you must do this without mockery or reproach, but with loving affection and a heart free from bitterness; not as if you were delivering a lecture or seeking the admiration of a bystander, but as if you were speaking to him alone, even if others are present.

Remember these nine precepts, as if received as a gift from the Muses, and begin at last to be a human being, while you live. But you must guard as much against flattering them as against being angry with them, for both are unsocial and lead to harm. And in your anger, have this thought ready: that to be enraged is not a manly quality, but that gentleness and civility are both more human and more manly.

The gentle man has strength, nerves, and Courage, not the indignant and discontented man. For the nearer a man is to Apatheia,[165] the nearer he is to power. Just as Distress is a mark of weakness, so is anger. For both have been wounded, and both have surrendered.

And if you will, take a tenth gift from the Leader of the Muses: to expect bad men not to do wrong is madness, for it is to wish for the impossible. But to allow them to be such toward others, and to demand that they do no wrong to you, is irrational and tyrannical.[166]

11.19 There are four deviations of your Ruling Faculty which you must constantly watch for and, when you detect them, suppress, saying to each:

"This Impression is unnecessary."

"This is destructive of Fellowship."

"What you are about to say is not from yourself."

And consider that to speak what is not from yourself is among the most absurd things.

And fourth, reproach yourself for this: that the more divine part in you is being defeated and bowing down to the more dishonored and mortal portion (that of the body) and to its gross pleasures.

11.20 Your little Pneuma and all the fire blended within you, though they by Nature tend upward, still obey the Administration of the Whole and are held fast here in the compound. And all that is earthy and liquid in you, though they naturally tend downward, are still raised up and stand in a position not their natural one. Thus the Elements obey the Whole: once posted somewhere under compulsion, they remain until the signal for Dissolution is given from there again.

Is it not a terrible thing, then, that the rational part of you alone should be disobedient and resent its place?

And yet little compulsion[167] is imposed upon it; only what is in accordance with its Nature. Still it does not submit, but is carried in the opposite direction.

Any movement toward injustice, intemperance, [anger,][168] Grief, or Fear is nothing but a desertion from Nature. And when the Ruling Faculty is resentful of anything that happens, it too is deserting its post. For it was made for Equity and Reverence no less than for Justice. These too are aspects of the universal Fellowship, and are even more ancient than just actions themselves.[169]

11.21 A man who does not have one and the same Goal of Life cannot be one and the same man throughout his life. But this is not enough, unless you add what that goal should be. For just as the conception of all goods is not the same for all, but only for some, so the goal must be a Social one, for the Common Good. He who directs all his own Impulses to this end will make all his actions alike, and so will always be the same.

11.22 The country mouse and the city mouse, and the terror and flight of the latter.[170]

11.23 Socrates called the opinions of the many "Lamias": bugbears for children.[171]

11.24 The Lacedaemonians[172] at their spectacles would set seats in the shade for their foreign guests, but they themselves sat wherever they could.

11.25 Socrates to Perdiccas, on why he did not visit him: "Lest I should die the most shameful of deaths." That is, lest I should receive a favor I could not repay.[173]

11.26 In the writings of the Ephesians[174] there was a precept to remember continually some of the ancients who practiced Virtue.

11.27 The Pythagoreans tell us to look at the sky at dawn, to remind ourselves of those beings that are always doing their own work in the same way, and of their Order, their purity, and their nakedness. For there is no veil for a star.[175]

11.28 What sort was Socrates, when he put on a sheepskin after Xanthippe[176] had taken his cloak and went out. What he said to his companions, who were ashamed and drew back when they saw him dressed that way.

11.29 In writing and reading, you will not lead until you have been led. Much more so in life.

11.30 "You are a slave by nature; you have no share in Reason."[177]

11.31 "And my own heart laughed within me."[178]

11.32 "And they will blame virtue with bitter words."[179]

11.33 To seek a fig in winter is madness. So is he who looks for his child who has passed.

11.34 When you kiss your child, said Epictetus, say to yourself: "Tomorrow you may be dead."

"These are words of ill omen."

"Nothing," he says, "can be of ill omen that is a Natural work. Or is it an ill omen to say that the ears of grain are reaped?"[180]

11.35 The grape, first unripe, then ripening, then a raisin. All are Transformations, not into Nothing, but into what is not yet.

11.36 "No one can rob us of our Moral Will," said Epictetus.[181]

11.37 He also said, "The art is to be found in the handling of Assent. And in the sphere of Impulse, be attentive that it is with a Reservation, that it is Social, and that it is according to worth."

He said that we should abstain from Desire altogether, and not be averse to any of those things that are not in our power.

11.38 "The contest," he said, "is not for some trivial prize, but for sanity or madness."[182]

11.39 Socrates used to say: "What do you want? The Psyches of Rational beings, or Irrational ones?"

Rational.

"What kind of Rational Psyches? Healthy or Corrupt?"

Healthy.

"Then why do you not seek them?"

Because we have them.

"Then why do you fight and disagree?"[183]

12

Book 12

MARCUS ANTONINUS EMPEROR: To Himself. Book 12.

12.1 All that you hope to attain by a roundabout course, you can have now, if you will not deny it to yourself. That is, if you release all of the past, entrust the future to Providence, and devote the present only to Reverence and Justice.

Reverence, that you may love what is allotted to you, for Nature brought it to you and you to it; and Justice, that you may speak the truth freely and without concealment, and act according to law and worth.

Let neither another's Vice, nor his Opinion, nor his voice hinder you, nor the sensations of this encasing flesh; let the part that suffers attend to itself.

If, then, as you approach your departure, you disregard all else and honor only your own Ruling Faculty and the Divinity within, and fear not that you will cease to live, but rather that you may never begin to live in accordance with Nature: you will be a man worthy of the Cosmos that made you.

You will no longer be a stranger in your own land, marveling at daily events as if they were unexpected, nor hanging in suspense on this or that.

12.2 God sees all Ruling Faculties stripped bare of their material vessels, husks, and impurities. With his own Intellect alone he makes contact only with that which has flowed from himself into them and been channeled there.

If you too accustom yourself to this, you will free yourself from great distraction. For he who overlooks even the flesh surrounding him will hardly be occupied with clothing, house, reputation, and other such wrappings and stage props.

12.3 There are three things of which you are composed: a little body, a little Pneuma, and Intellect. The first two are under your care only insofar as you must tend them; the third alone is truly your own.

And if you separate from yourself (that is, from your Mind) all that others say or do, all that you have said or done, all future troubles, whatever belongs to the body placed around you[184] or the innate breath that is outside your Moral Will, and whatever the external swirling vortex whirls around; so that your Intellectual Power, removed from the things bound up with Fate, can live for itself, pure and free, doing what is just, accepting whatever comes, and speaking the truth; I say, you separate from this Ruling Faculty all that adheres to it from attachment,[185] and from time all that lies beyond or has passed, you will make yourself like the sphere of Empedocles, "a rounded sphere, rejoicing in its circular solitude."[186]

You will train yourself to live only what you are living; that is, the present. Then you will be able to live out the remainder of your days until death free from turmoil, nobly,[187] and at peace with your own Daimon.

12.4 I have often wondered why it is that, though every man loves himself more than all others, he should value his own opinion of himself less than that of others. For if a God or a wise teacher were to stand at a man's side and command him to think or conceive of nothing inwardly without at once speaking it aloud, he would not endure it for even a single day. Thus we stand in greater awe of what our neighbors will think of us than of what we think of ourselves.

12.5 How is it that the Gods, having ordered all things rightly and with love for mankind, have overlooked this one thing alone: that certain men, exceedingly good, who have made the most numerous contracts, as it were, with the divine, and have become most intimate with it through pious acts and sacred rites; once they have died, no longer come into being again, but are utterly extinguished?

Now, if this is indeed so, be assured that if it ought to have been otherwise, they would have made it so. For if it were Just, it would also be possible; and if it were according to Nature, Nature would have brought it to pass. From the fact that it is not so (if indeed it is not so) let this convince you that it ought not to have been so. For you see yourself that in raising this objection you are pleading a case against God; and we would not be reasoning with the Gods in this way if they were not supremely good and most Just. But if they are, they would not have overlooked anything in the ordering of the Cosmos left neglected through injustice or unreason.

12.6 Practice even those things you despair of. For the left hand, which is ineffective for other things through lack of practice, grips the reins more firmly than the right, for it has been practiced in this.

12.7 Consider in what state one must be overtaken by death, both in Body and in Psyche. The brevity of life. The yawning vastness of Eternity before and after. The weakness of all Matter.

12.8 To behold the Causal Elements stripped naked of their coverings; the references of actions; what is Pain, what is Pleasure, what is death, what is glory; who is the author of his own unrest; how no one is hindered by another; that all is Judgment.

12.9 In applying your principles, you must be like the pancratiast, not the gladiator. For the gladiator lays down the sword he uses and takes it up again; but the pancratiast always has his hand, and need do nothing but clench it.[188]

12.10 To observe things as such, dividing them into Matter, Cause, and

Purpose.

12.11 What power man has! To do nothing other than what God will approve, and to welcome all that God allots to him.

12.12 Neither are the Gods to be blamed, for they err in nothing, whether willingly or unwillingly, nor men, for they err in nothing except unwillingly. Therefore no one is to be blamed.

12.13 How ridiculous and strange is the man who is surprised by anything that happens in life.

12.14 Either a fated Necessity and an inviolable order, or a Providence open to supplication, or a leaderless jumble of randomness. If an inviolable Necessity, why do you resist? If a Providence admitting of propitiation, make yourself worthy of the aid from the divine. If an ungoverned confusion, take heart that in such a flood you yourself have within you a governing Intellect. And if the flood should carry you away, let it carry away the paltry flesh, the paltry Pneuma, and all the rest; for the Intellect it will not carry away.

12.15 Does the light of a lamp shine until it is extinguished without losing its radiance? And shall the Truth, Justice, and Temperance within you be extinguished before you are?

12.16 In the case of one who has furnished the Impression that he has erred: how indeed do I know that this is an error?

And even if he has erred, he has condemned himself, and this is like clawing at his own face. He who would not have the base man err is like one who would not have the fig-tree produce its juice in the figs, or infants whimper, or the horse neigh, or any other necessary thing. For what can he be expected to suffer, having such a disposition?

If then you are so keen, cure it.

12.17 If it is not fitting, do not do it; if it is not true, do not say it.

12.18 Let your Impulse be directed toward always examining what that very thing is that produces the Impression in you, and to unfold it by dividing it into the Cause, the Material, the Purpose, and the time within which it must cease.

12.19 Realize at last that you have something in you more powerful and more divine than what causes the Passions and pulls you like a puppet. What is my Mind now? Surely not Fear? Surely not suspicion? Surely not Desire? Surely not something of that sort?

12.20 First, do nothing at random, nor without a purpose. Second, let your purpose be nothing other than the Common Good.

12.21 In a little while you will be no one and nowhere, nor will any of the things you now see exist, nor any of those who are now living. For all things are by nature subject to Transformation, to Alteration, and to Decay, so that other things may arise in their place.

12.22 All is Judgment, and that is in your power. Remove your Judgment, then, when you choose, and like one who has rounded the cape, there is calm, all things steady, and a waveless bay.

12.23 Any single action whatsoever, by ceasing at its proper time, suffers no evil by the fact that it has ceased; nor does the one who performed this action suffer any evil by this very fact: that it has ceased. Likewise, then, the whole system of actions, which is life, if it ceases at its proper time, suffers no evil by this very fact: that it has ceased; nor is he who brings this chain to a timely end badly disposed. But the time and the limit are given by Nature: sometimes by one's own nature, as in old age; but always by the Nature of the Whole, by the transforming of whose parts the entire Cosmos remains ever young and in its prime. And always beautiful and seasonable is everything that is beneficial to the Whole. Therefore, the cessation of life is no evil for each individual, since it is not even shameful, if indeed it is outside the sphere of Moral Will and not detrimental to the Common Good. Rather, it is a good, if it is seasonable and advantageous to the Whole, and being carried along in accord with it. For thus also is one God-borne who is carried toward the same things as God, being borne toward the same things in purpose.

12.24 It is necessary to keep these three things ready to hand. First, concerning your actions: consider whether they are done neither at random nor otherwise than as Justice herself would have acted; and concerning external events, that they happen either by contingency or by Providence, and one should neither blame contingency nor accuse Providence.

Second: consider what each thing is from seed until receiving the Psyche, and from receiving the Psyche until the giving back of the Psyche; and from what things its Composition arises, and into what its Dissolution returns.

Third: if you were suddenly raised aloft and looked down on human affairs and their variety, you would despise them, perceiving at the same time how great is the surrounding host of aerial and ethereal beings; and that however often you might be raised up, you would see the same things: all of one form, all of short duration.

Upon such things rests our vanity!

12.25 Cast out the Judgment, and you are saved. Who then is there to prevent you from casting it out?

12.26 When you are troubled by anything, you have forgotten that all things come about according to the Nature of the Whole, and that the wrong done is another's. And this besides: that everything that happens has always happened so, and will happen so, and is now happening so everywhere. You have forgotten how great the kinship of man is with the whole human race; for it is not a communion of mere blood or mere seed, but of Intellect. And you have forgotten this too: that the Intellect of each person is God, and has flowed from thence; that nothing is anyone's own, but that even our little child, our little body, our very little Psyche have come from thence; that all things are Judgment; and that each of us lives only the Present, and this is all he loses.

12.27 Constantly call to mind those who have been mightily indignant about something, those who have reached the greatest heights of fame, or misfortune, or enmity, or any other fate. Then stop and ask: where is it all now? Smoke and ash and a tale, or not even a tale. Let all such examples come to mind: Fabius Catullinus on his country estate, Lusius Lupus [in his gardens],[189] Stertinius at Baiae, Tiberius at Capri, Velius Rufus.[190] And in general, consider the eager pursuit of anything with vanity. How much cheaper is all that we strive for, and how much more philosophical to show oneself Just, Temperate, and an obedient follower of the Gods in the matter given you, and to do it with simplicity. For the pride that prides itself on its lack of pride is the most intolerable of all.

12.28 To those who ask, "Where have you seen the Gods, or how have you apprehended that they exist, that you worship them so?"

I answer: first, they are visible even to the eye; second, I have not seen my own Psyche, and yet I honor it. So too with the Gods: from my constant experience of their power, I apprehend that they exist, and I revere them.

12.29 The security of life is to see each thing for what it is, in its entirety: what in it is Material and what is Causal; to do what is Just and to speak the truth with all one's Psyche. What remains but to enjoy life, joining one good thing to another so as to leave not the smallest interval between?

12.30 There is one light of the sun, though it is divided by walls, mountains, and countless other things. There is one common Substance, though it is divided among countless individually qualified bodies. There is one Psyche, though it is divided among countless natures and individual circumscriptions. There is one Intellectual Psyche, though it seems to have been separated. Now the other parts of the things mentioned, such as breaths and substrates, are without perception and without mutual affinity; yet even these are held together by the unifying principle and by their tendency to gravitate toward the same. But Mind strains particularly toward what is of its own kind, and combines with it, and the Social affection is not divided.

12.31 What do you seek after? To breathe? Or rather, to perceive? To have Impulses? To grow? To cease again? To use your voice? To think? Which of these seems to you worthy of desire?

But if each of these is contemptible, proceed to the final thing: to follow Reason and God. But it conflicts with honoring these to be troubled that through dying one will be deprived of those other things.

12.32 How small a portion of infinite and boundless Eternity has been apportioned to each of us, for most swiftly it is swallowed up in the Everlasting. How small a portion of the whole Substance; how small a portion of the universal Psyche. And on what a tiny clod of the whole earth do you crawl! Reflecting on all this, conceive of nothing as great except this: to act as your own Nature leads, and to bear what Common Nature brings.

12.33 How does the Ruling Faculty employ itself? For in this lies everything. The remaining things, whether objects of Moral Will or not, are dead things and smoke.

12.34 Most rousing toward a contempt of death is this: that even those who judged Pleasure to be a Good and Pain an Evil have nevertheless despised it.

12.35 He to whom that alone is good which is timely, and to whom it is equal whether he has performed a greater or lesser number of actions in accordance with right Reason, and for whom it makes no difference whether he contemplates the Cosmos for a longer or shorter time; for this man, death is nothing to be feared.

12.36 Man, you have been a citizen in this Great City. What does it matter to you whether for five years or three?

For what is according to the laws is equal for all.

What is terrible, then, if you are sent out of the city, not by a tyrant or an unjust judge, but by the Nature that brought you in?

It is as if a comic actor were dismissed from the stage by the praetor who engaged him.

"But I have not played the five acts, only three."[191]

You speak well; but in life, three acts are the whole play. For he sets the end who was once the cause of its Composition, and is now of its Dissolution. You are the cause of neither. Depart, then, with a good grace, for he who dismisses you is also gracious.

The End of the Books of Marcus Antoninus, Philosopher and Emperor, Concerning His Own Life.

Xylander's Dedicatory Epistle

Note: This is the dedicatory letter from Wilhelm Xylander's 1558/59 Latin edition of Marcus Aurelius's *Meditations*, addressed to Georg von Stetten the Younger, a patrician of Augsburg.

Xylander dedicates his Latin translation of the *Meditations* to Georg von Stetten the Younger, a patrician of Augsburg, out of personal gratitude and to lend the edition credibility.

He praises Marcus as both philosopher and emperor, sketches his character from ancient sources, and then turns refreshingly candid about the work itself: the Greek manuscript was damaged and incomplete, the translation was grueling, and he sometimes had to guess at the meaning or depart boldly from the text.

He defends publishing an imperfect edition over letting the work remain unknown.

* * *

To the truly noble Georg von Stetten the Younger, Patrician of Augsburg, to be honored with the highest regard, Guilielmus Xylander of Augsburg sends greetings.

When I had made a Latin translation of this little work of M. ANTONINUS, Roman Emperor, he who is called the Philosopher, at the urging of CONRAD GESSNER, most distinguished physician and philosopher, and a man joined to me by the closest friendship, and when the edition of this little work was already being prepared, not one reason alone impelled me to inscribe it to your most illustrious name, most distinguished Sir. For I saw that I could publicly testify how gratefully I cherished the memory of your goodwill toward me (which I experienced in the fullest measure, both on other occasions and especially last May in person in our homeland); and I judged that the splendor of your name would bring no small favor to this very edition. Now, since I was well enough assured what your devotion to the study of wisdom was, and your feeling about those disciplines that pertain to humane learning, and with what diligence you had been engaged in them from an early age, and that you had always embraced the cultivators of those arts and their followers with goodness: I did not fear that you would not find this service of mine, whatever its quality, agreeable. The book itself, both by the dignity of its author and by the excellence of the subject it treats, will easily win from you that you deem it worthy of your protection. Of my own labor I shall speak afterward.

That this little work was written by ANTONINUS the Philosopher Emperor, we demonstrate in our annotations: so that it is not at all necessary to repeat here what we have said there. But that this great Emperor meditated upon the chief topics of Philosophy with himself, and pondered them diligently, you will discover for yourself either from our words or, if you prefer, from the Greek when you read it. For even if it is true that these books of ANTONINUS (as indeed they have come into our hands) are mutilated, wretchedly and for the greater part cut short, nevertheless it is readily apparent that there remain in them the weightiest discussions concerning the endurance of the human condition, the contempt of death, the preservation of human society, true happiness, the causes of human miseries, and other topics of Philosophy of this kind in great number, and these discussions refined with arguments both acute and furnished with the most fitting examples and comparisons. Nor is the manner of philosophizing of our author unlike that which Epictetus is known to have used (who preceded ANTONINUS in age by not very long, and whose use of his own precepts our author openly acknowledges) as Arrian committed to record. For around that time the pursuit of wisdom flourished to such a degree that the Emperors themselves either cultivated philosophy or at least did not scorn its adherents. Whence it came about that there existed very many men outstanding in learning and gravity, of whom the names and sayings and deeds of some survive among the writers of history, while the writings of others, most learned and full of wisdom, have endured to our own age.

Indeed, I judge ANTONINUS (nor do I think the learned feel otherwise) to have intended in these Commentaries not merely to set forth the matters with which he himself occupied his mind, and by what precepts, examples, and reasonings he had shaped himself to maintain with dignity the name of a man, a citizen, an Emperor, and indeed a Philosopher; but also to have demonstrated what was the true and ready path to tranquillity of mind, and to that happiness which can fall to a man's lot in this life to attain; and then, whatever the reason might be, why most men so undeservedly complained about nature and their own fortune. For in this way philosophy, neglected and despised, takes vengeance upon them: whose complaint and indignation the most wise Poet Euripides expressed with as much skill and (as in all things) elegance, bringing onto the stage an old man struck by calamity, who, since he had reckoned too little the principles for living at the very time when he most ought to have done so, when he fell into adversity, did not recognize the fault of his own imprudence, but (as is the way of the common crowd) took refuge in futile and useless prayers. Concerning whose ignorance there exist these verses, which I shall adduce, rendered by me into Latin, however, lest I insert foreign speech into this kind of discourse:

Alas, that this is not granted to mortals, That the young might be young twice, and the old again? For if at home something should chance to go amiss, We correct it nonetheless with fresh counsel: But life one cannot retrace. Yet if youth Were to return, and old age were twofold, We would correct the sins of this life, Having better foreseen a new course of living.

A capital fool, this Iphis, and deserving of any misfortune, who would not guide his present life rightly by precepts and examples, but would wish instead for something else by which the errors of his life might be corrected. How much more rightly did Theseus, that Euripidean character, whose saying Cicero reports as his own:

For I, who had heard these things from a learned man, Used to ponder future miseries with myself: Either bitter death, or the sorrowful flight of exile, Or always some burden of evil I was meditating, So that if some dire calamity should come upon me by chance, No unexpected care should tear me unawares.

But that this ordering of life is to be sought from philosophy is not obscure, and has been so demonstrated by many other weighty authors that the matter needs neither my words nor time in this place. This indeed I do not think it rash to add: that the method of philosophizing which our author maintained (that is, which he carried out by means of brief precepts, examples, and comparisons) is, for the greater part of mankind, both easier to understand and more convenient to retain in memory than that other method which extracts truth through exquisite disputations and ingenious conclusions. Which itself tends toward this end: that it may be understood what the present book can contribute to the shaping of the common life of men.

But I pass over commending the book, especially since, once begun, it easily retains the reader; so that I do not doubt it will prove true in this case, as that same Poet aptly said: that the buyer, once having had a taste, is enticed. Concerning my labor and the effort I applied in translating, it remains for me to speak: although I would rather leave my fidelity and diligence to be assessed by the learned through a comparison made of the Greek with the Latin book than boast of myself or my work. Nor indeed do I fear that anyone will attack this edition, unless there are those who will indignantly refuse to have a book that is mutilated and in many places interrupted and interpolated offered to readers. Whom I shall then consider worth hearing, if they themselves produce a more complete version: otherwise, if they are to be judged learned by that standard, they will bring it about that we disregard the remnants of good books, which themselves we rightly value highly. Indeed, if our forebears had held the same judgment concerning fragments of books or mutilated volumes, good God, how many and how splendid and useful books we would not have today! But farewell to such captious critics.

To be sure, this task of translating has grown upon me wonderfully: and

I hardly know whether I would have abandoned the undertaking, had not a certain necessity, born of the obligation I had given not to betray my good faith and my sense of honor, and of my purpose (which is to serve the Republic of Letters to the best of my ability, and for that reason to yield to no labor or be willing to succumb to any) confirmed me in persevering. I strove for the best Latinity I could achieve in this business, except that I did not scorn certain words, familiar and apt ones, though not commonly used among the ancients, for the sake of clarity. I neither wished nor indeed ought to have weighed my words on a jeweler's scale: I have followed the sense, but whether I have everywhere attained it, I desire the judgment of others. Why this should have been difficult, the reasons are many and not hidden. And I confess that in certain passages I may have needed either to divine the meaning or to have departed boldly from the Greek text or from common usage: in which places, although I have sometimes offered help through brief annotations (for I was busier than leisure for commenting would allow), nevertheless if anyone should think otherwise, I am not troubled: for, as the proverb of Bacchylides has it, the road is wide.

But to you, most excellent Sir, why I have dedicated this book and the labor I have spent upon it, and why I have deemed neither unworthy of the patronage of your eminence, I have already recounted above. It remained for me to ask you not to disdain this effort of mine to adorn your name and to declare the gratitude of my spirit toward you: but so great is your humanity, and your love toward the defenders and promoters of literary endeavor (among whom I should wish to be counted even in the last place), that I may assuredly promise myself of you that I need not, by beseeching, call your goodness into doubt. Therefore I perceive that I may dispense with the labor of entreating you. I commend myself to you, whom I know as a singular ornament of our most illustrious homeland, and a most benevolent patron of the Muses, and I commend my studies to you, and I shall see to it, unless something human should befall us too soon, that your goodwill toward me shall not cause you regret.

Farewell. Heidelberg, the Kalends [first] of October, in the Year of Salvation 1558.

An engraved portrait of Wilhelm Xylander, circa 1628, possibly by French engraver Robert Boissard. The engraved text reads: "Greece would owe the most to Xylander, were it not that Plutarch himself already wears the Roman toga."
The handwritten text reads: "Born in Augsburg, Professor of the Greek language in Heidelberg, published Theocritus, Stephanus Byzantinus, Horace, [unclear]; translated into Latin Dio Cassius, Marcus Aurelius, Antoninus Liberalis, Phlegon, Antigonus of Carystus, Plutarch's Moralia, Strabo, etc."
Reproduced from an original print in the translator's personal collection.

136

Conrad Gessner's Greek Dedicatory Epistle

Note: This is a translation of Conrad Gessner's Greek Dedicatory Epistle. This dedicatory letter, was written in Greek by Conrad Gessner to Anton Werther von Bechlingen. This letter precedes the Greek section of Xylander's *editio princeps*.

* * *

To the most noble Anton Bertram von Bechlingen, Conrad Gessner wishes well, with God's help.

True and sincere theology, most noble BERTRAM, and the accurate account of human happiness, immediately after the creation of the world, as you yourself know, God revealed to the forefather and progenitor of us all, the first formed man, and through him was pleased to make it known. Then to Seth, and to Enoch, and to Noah, and to the rest of the patriarchs, as successors of that divine inheritance: until after a considerable time God more clearly promised to the most pious Abraham that which surpasses human nature, having at the same time bestowed a sign of circumcision, a seal of the righteousness of faith: namely, that from his offspring the Savior of our race was foreordained to be born. Afterward again to Moses, the leader of the Jews, the foundations of all worship and priestly ministry were renewed. And last of all, our Lord and Savior JESUS Christ, the Son of God, taking on flesh like ours, and having dwelt among men for a long time, by words of divine teaching and by wondrous works, by his whole life, and by death on our behalf on the third day, confirmed the truth of these things, having risen again, so that whoever after these events does not still believe in Him, and does not still question Him, and does not hearken to Him, should seem to me ungodly. And this is the Wisdom handed down to us from this teacher: which not only engages in the contemplation of divine things, but also governs human affairs and actions, and shows those who truly emulate these things to be truly happy: and it becomes the cause of genuine happiness not only to individuals in private, but also to households and cities.

Beside this, when one examines the doctrines of philosophy and theology among the Greeks and other nations, the greater part appears to be nonsense and idle talk (as the ancient one wisely declared, that the Greeks are always children); and some of it even appears to be godlessness and impiety. For to pass over countless other matters in silence, concerning the different parts of philosophy which are drawn from the sacred books of our faith, these are set forth most correctly and clearly: and nearly all the pagan philosophers, disagreeing with one another on most things, agree on this one point (which is indeed the greatest error of all), namely concerning the nature of true happiness both in the present life and after the separation of the soul from the body, the principle and root of which is in us and comes from us. But the leader and teacher of our theology, JESUS Christ, has shown to mankind the source and foundation of His own blessedness, and has laid it down plainly, and has made us His own: showing us not only how to bear the condition of piety, that is, the required and necessary faith, which is both the first and most firmly established, all things having been prophesied from the beginning through the divine prophetic men, and then through CHRIST and the Apostles and other saints assembled together, as most true; and the chief point of all their teaching is this: that the Savior (who, on account of the weakness of nature, and of the law which came from it, and of all to which it was subject) came down from divine grace to mankind, not indeed through some mediator or friend toward Him (for it is impossible; and the mediator of this is only He who was revealed without sin as the Savior, who alone partakes of both natures), of divine and human; but this mystery which the wise men among the Greeks were unable to express, and besides countless other things, concerning the gods themselves they turned away, full of myths and impiety, being brought to ruin: and they endanger not only those others, but also many of those who profess to be Christians, concerning the principle of these things which are beyond the power of human nature, as being of value, since only through the Mediator (who imparts His own righteousness and perfection to us, and through His own blood washes away our transgressions) is the confirmation of all true happiness and the turning toward the divine achieved, which through Him alone is simply and comprehensively established, provided that one sins moderately. For once a beginning is made of any kind of error, what follows always proceeds toward what is worse, and manifold error comes to deceive everyone. So that we see among both the Greeks and others, on account of this, the doctrines of those who philosophized in former times to be innumerable, contrary to one another, and entirely alien to true piety.

Let it be clear that those who are good in their zeal and disposition toward one another for the sake of the virtues befitting man (those virtues themselves being) constitutive of happiness, as the Stoics held, both others and Seneca and Epictetus; and he who after them was most distinguished in this wisdom, the Emperor Antoninus, the Philosopher. For if nothing else were a friend of this school (namely, that human wisdom is the best and most perfect of all for the attainment of happiness, and the mind, as it were, is everything, as some would persuade us), yet it becomes a kind of tutor to us, leading us to the recognition of our own weakness, as also the Old Covenant of our faith, concerning the law and human actions. For starting from this very point and being, as it were, trained by it, and using it as a provision (since, being incomplete, and finding all our thoughts and deeds mixed with disturbance and passion), we no longer find the solution in ourselves, but outside ourselves, and above us we must seek perfection: just as those who are sick in body, first trying whether it is possible to be restored by means of nature, spend time recovering; then, when they are not helped, and perhaps even grow worse, as if the nature of their illness and disease were not within themselves to cure, they come to seek external remedies and the prescriptions of a physician. But enough of these things for now.

Concerning the author himself of these memoranda, it is now time to say something. The name of "Philosopher" befits the Emperor Antoninus, and it seems to me very fitting: for they define philosophy as the knowledge of divine and human things, insofar as it is attainable by man. And the Emperor seems to have arrived at the summit of wisdom, that is, of human and especially moral wisdom. For he was wonderfully well disposed by nature toward all the virtues, and in his soul he surpassed nearly all men in moderation, that is, in being disposed moderately or even impassibly toward all that befalls one.

But how could one who is ignorant of Christ, the crowning point of all virtue, surpass most of those who possess the treasures of our piety, even in moderation of passion and in nearly all the virtues of character: justice, temperance, endurance, kindness, gentleness, and others? Is it not that the summit and peak of happiness, being a gift from above, lies in those very virtues, and that one who is persuaded of this strives to live virtuously and contends toward these things with all zeal and power? But the Christians, knowing the divine grace and mercy, and that the passions of human weakness are naturally implanted in them, do not attempt simply to strip these away entirely. For most people are very weak even in these matters. But if one would not otherwise attain happiness unless one had mastered these things, as Antoninus more diligently practiced his devotion: but knowing that even if we should fall short of the divine commands, we are still useful, and that we have done nothing beyond what is required, and if we do what is needful according to the capacity of human nature, that God will visit us with His kindness and grace through His own goodness, which many think it is less important to have. Wherever it may be, one who praises not simply, but nonetheless gives an account through this discourse, for even the sinner, that tax collector who stood in the temple and did not dare to raise his eyes to heaven, but beat his breast and said to himself, "God, be merciful to me, the sinner," went away more justified than the Pharisee, who thought himself righteous as having kept all the commandments. For human righteousness, even if it seems to have reached the utmost perfection, if it claims worthiness for itself, by this very presumption it will thoroughly cast itself down as wholly unworthy. But one must hold noble and prudent actions toward virtue as, so to speak, fruits, bearing witness to the hidden root of faith, as testimony of the faith that saves, so that God, in what He has done for us, may be glorified in trust; and as for the faithless and impious, let it be so: we entrust the hearts of all men and all people to God, whether...

...having found these active in us, we imitate Him whom we recall among our fathers in heaven. Let each one love and imitate what he will.

But let me return to my discourse about Antoninus, the Philosopher Emperor. These books I came upon, well and beautifully written, in the possession of Michael Toxites, a poet of excellent natural gifts (from the library of Count Heinrich of the Palatinate, the most splendid library), and having obtained them through our care in a fitting manner, I now first present them in print, dedicating them to your Excellency and offering them, most noble BERTRAM, for good reasons.

For of your piety and sense of justice (to say nothing of your other virtues) I have heard not only from many who attest to them, but I myself have experienced them firsthand, as a guest in your city of Zurich. And it seemed to me altogether fitting that these most royal and wise memoranda should be addressed and dedicated to one who happens to be not merely of noble birth and great soul, but also not inexperienced in philosophy and the Greek language. And you, most excellent one, appeared to us at just the right moment, as if sent by God (as the saying goes, from the machine), present to all of us, as I shall show. For you happen to be both well born and of distinguished family, if any man is; and in learning (in the books of both Romans and Greeks) and in the education of wisdom you have engaged not moderately (beyond all, at least, those whom we have found to be of both our own birth and fortune similarly), as also your two brothers, teachers among the most learned of men, and having met the very distinguished GEORG FABRICIUS. Receive therefore, most excellent BERTRAM, this imperial gift graciously and kindly: and enjoy the golden treasure of its many good things for your benefit. For good men, those who are also of God, wise men, profit from all things, and all things turn to their good. Since, as to what I shall say, that is, as those who have been emboldened by their own actions before God, they do nothing superfluous. But they do all things for the sake of

God's glory: not as base slaves demanding a reward, but as those who do all things freely through CHRIST, acting in freedom as toward GOD as Father, expecting favor and paternal reward from the better things, without any doubt. I know well that this little book will be pleasing to you: first because it both teaches about matters of the greatest importance in a manner that is elsewhere also remarkable (concerning virtue and education, concerning the avoidance of error, or rather concerning the providence of God, and how through it all things must sustain us, and since willingly and without hesitation, wherever such men may be, and surpassing most others, wise men) let it be known that such a writing was found almost by chance, and unless it had been published in his own handwriting. For from nearly all the Caesars and Emperors nothing else has come to us that was written by them.

FAREWELL, and greet your excellent brothers Volgang and Philip from me, embracing them most warmly as sharers in the Antonine books above all. From the city of Zurich, first among the Helvetians, in the year of salvation 1559, in the middle of the month of February.

From the Suda

Note: These are excerpts about Marcus Aurelius from ancient sources, presented by Xylander as introductory material. This was presented in both Latin and Greek. This translation is sourced from the Greek version.

***

FROM THE SUDA

Marcus, also known as Antoninus, King of the Romans, praised in all things as a Philosopher, having been a student of various teachers, and later a devoted follower of Sextus, the Boeotian philosopher, at Rome, admiring him and frequenting his doors. To him came Lucius, an acquaintance and orator, a relation of Herodes the Athenian orator, and finding him thus engaged, said: "Where is the King going, and for what purpose?" And Marcus said: "It is good even for one growing old to learn. I am going to Sextus the philosopher to learn what I do not yet know." And Lucius, raising his hand toward heaven, said: "O Sun! The King of the Romans, now an old man, taking up his tablet, goes to a teacher's school!"

My own emperor Alexander died at the age of thirty two. This man wrote about himself in twelve books.

AND AGAIN

Marcus, King of the Romans: whom one would more fittingly honor with silence than praise readily, since no account is worthy of the man's virtues. For from the very beginning of his youth, being of a calm and quiet disposition, he never turned his face to pleasure at any time. He praised among the philosophers those from the Stoic school. And he was an imitator of those men, not only in the resolution of problems but also in the comprehension of their teachings. Thus from youth through the middle of his life he shone so brightly that Hadrian often wished to appoint this man as heir to the imperial succession. But since he had already adopted Pius according to the law as his predecessor, he preserved the succession for that one; but this man he came to know through the bond of marriage with Pius, so that through the succession of his family he might come to the throne. For both in his private life and in his public life among the Romans, he was in no way altered by the change of his position: and when he came to the rule and the monarchy, being justly governed, and enduring the utmost hardship, he never at any time gave way to any arrogance. But he was free and generous in his benefactions: good and moderate in the administration of the affairs of nations.

From the Epitome of Sextus Aurelius Victor

Note: This is a translation of the excerpt from the *Epitome de Caesaribus* attributed to Sextus Aurelius Victor, a late Roman biographical compendium. Xylander included this brief historical account of Marcus Aurelius's reign as introductory material in his 1558/59 edition, presented in Latin.

* * *

Antoninus ruled for eighteen years. He was a man of heavenly character in all virtues, and was set forth as a kind of defender against public calamities. For indeed, had he not been born for those times, assuredly all the affairs of the Roman state would have collapsed as if in a single fall. For there was never rest from arms: and throughout the entire East, Illyricum, Italy, and Gaul wars raged; there were earthquakes, not without the destruction of cities, floods of rivers, frequent plagues, a species of locusts infesting the fields: in short, there is scarcely anything by which mortals are customarily afflicted with the greatest distresses that can be named or imagined which did not rage during his reign. He admitted his kinsman L. Annius Verus to a share of the empire by a new kind of benevolence. This Verus, while traveling between Altinum and Concordia, was struck down by a rush of blood, the disease which the Greeks call ἀποπληξία [apoplexia], in the eleventh year of the reign. He was most devoted to Tragic poetry, of a harsh and wanton character. After his death, M. Antoninus held the Republic alone, from the beginning of his life the most tranquil of men, so much so that from infancy he never changed his expression either from joy or from sorrow, devoted to philosophy, most skilled in Greek literature. He permitted men of distinction to hold banquets with the same style of service as he himself used, and with similar attendants. When the treasury was exhausted and he did not have the funds to bestow upon the soldiers, and was unwilling to impose any levy upon the provincials or the Senate, he held a sale in the forum of Trajan of the furnishings of the imperial household: golden vessels, crystal and murrhine cups, his wife's and his own silk and gold clothing, many ornaments of gems: and for two continuous months the sale was held, and much gold was collected. After the victory, however, he returned the prices to the buyers who wished to give back what they had purchased. He was a burden to no one who preferred to keep what he had once bought. In his time Cassius, seizing at tyranny, was destroyed. He himself in the fifty ninth year of his life was consumed by disease at Vindobona. When the news of his death reached Rome, the city was thrown into confusion by public mourning; the Senate, dressed in dark clothing, met in the Curia weeping. And what was reluctantly believed of Romulus, all with equal feeling presumed: that Marcus had been received into heaven. In his honor temples, columns, and many other things were decreed.

Translation and Terminology Glossary

Reading ancient philosophy in translation presents some interesting challenges. The words on the page appear familiar ("soul," "spirit," "nature," "reason") yet they carry meanings shaped by two thousand years of intellectual history that separates us from the original authors. When Marcus Aurelius wrote of his *psychē*, he meant something quite specific: a material entity composed of refined fire and air, located in his chest, capable of dissolving entirely at death. When a modern reader encounters "soul" in translation, they almost inevitably import concepts of immortality, immateriality, and divine judgment that would have been foreign to Stoic thought.

This translation addresses that problem through two related strategies. First, where no English word adequately captures the Greek meaning without distortion, the Greek term is retained in transliterated form: Psyche rather than "soul," Pneuma rather than "spirit," Daimon rather than "inner spirit." Second, where English words can serve but require disambiguation from their ordinary usage, they are systematically capitalized: Nature (the cosmic rational principle) versus nature (individual character), Reason (the divine intelligence ordering the Cosmos) versus reason (ordinary thinking).

Beyond terminology, this translation aims to present the text as Marcus wrote it: in the language and conceptual framework of second-century Stoic philosophy, without the distortions introduced by two millennia of Christian theology, Victorian propriety, or modern paraphrase. The *Meditations* were composed in Koine Greek by a Roman emperor on military campaign, written as private philosophical notebooks never intended for publication. They are raw, repetitive, sometimes fragmentary, and unflinchingly honest. Where Marcus is blunt, this translation is blunt. Where his attitudes reflect the realities of ancient Roman life, slavery, gladiatorial combat, the omnipresence of death, the frank assessment of bodily decay, this translation lets him speak without apology or anachronistic moral commentary.

The glossary that follows explains the key terms and the rationale behind their treatment. It is organized in six parts: untranslated Greek terms, capitalized English translations, key phrases, a note on Stoic materialism, a note on the identity of divine concepts, and a comparison of existing translations. Readers may wish to consult it before beginning the translation, or return to it as unfamiliar terms arise.

Translation Philosophy

Three principles govern this translation: literal fidelity to the Greek, philosophical precision in terminology, and no censorship. The preceding chapters discuss the first and third; the glossary that follows addresses the second.

1. Untranslated Greek Terms

Psyche (ψυχή)

The animating principle of living beings; in humans, the seat of consciousness, reason, and identity.

The English word "soul" cannot serve here because it carries theological implications incompatible with Stoic philosophy. For most English speakers, "soul" suggests an immaterial substance, immortal by nature, destined for judgment after death, and fundamentally distinct from the body it inhabits. Stoic *psyche* is none of these things. It is material, composed of Pneuma, a refined mixture of fire and air. It is corporeal, possessing physical extension and capable of acting upon and being acted upon by other bodies. Most importantly, it may dissolve entirely at death, its constituent elements dispersing back into the cosmic Whole.

Marcus returns repeatedly to the question of whether Psyches persist after death or simply disperse. This is a question that would make no sense if *psychē* meant what "soul" means in Christian theology. By retaining the Greek term, this translation preserves both the philosophical content of Marcus's reflections and the genuine uncertainty he expresses about postmortem survival.

Pneuma (πνεῦμα)

The material substance, a dynamic mixture of fire and air, that pervades and animates the entire Cosmos.

In Stoic physics, Pneuma is the "stuff" of which Psyche, Reason, and even God are composed. It provides tension, cohesion, and vitality to all things, binding the Cosmos into a living, organic whole. The English "spirit" inevitably suggests immaterial substances, ghostly entities, and the Holy Spirit of Christian theology, which are precisely the associations that would obscure Pneuma's essential corporeality. Stoic Pneuma is a physical substance, however refined, and calling it "spirit" would import the dualistic metaphysics that Stoicism explicitly rejects. "Pneuma" is already naturalized in English through words like "pneumatic" and "pneumonia," and its retention signals to the reader that something more precise than "spirit" or "breath" is at work.

Daimon (δαίμων)

The divine rational principle dwelling within each person; one's portion of cosmic Reason.

The Greek *daimōn* is a specifically Greco-Roman concept: a divine or semi-divine presence, benevolent in nature, associated with one's fate and rational guidance. English "demon" has become entirely negative, suggesting evil supernatural beings, the opposite of the Greek meaning. "Inner spirit" introduces the same problems discussed above while adding vagueness. The Daimon is essentially identical with what Stoics call the Ruling Faculty (*hēgemonikon*) when that faculty is considered in its divine aspect: the fragment of cosmic Reason that constitutes each person's truest self. "Daimon" has established precedent in English philosophical writing (most famously in discussions of Socrates's *daimonion*) and carries no misleading theological baggage.

Apatheia (ἀπάθεια)

The Stoic ideal of freedom from destructive, irrational emotions; equanimity achieved through rational mastery.

Modern English "apathy" means indifference, lack of interest, or emotional deadness, the opposite of what Stoics valued. Stoic Apatheia is not the absence of all feeling but specifically the elimination of the irrational *pathē* (Desire, Fear, Pleasure, and Distress) that disturb the Psyche's proper functioning. The Stoic sage still experiences what Stoic philosophers called the *eupatheiai*, the rational emotions of Joy, Wish, and Caution. Where this concept appears, "Apatheia" or "absence of Passions" preserves the technical meaning.

2. Capitalized English Terms

The terms in this section have adequate English translations but are capitalized to distinguish their technical Stoic usage from ordinary meanings. When you encounter "Nature" with a capital N, this signals the cosmic rational principle, not merely the physical world or someone's character.

The Divine and the Cosmos

Nature (*physis*, φύσις): The rational ordering principle of the Cosmos, identical with God, Reason, Fate, and Providence. Universal Nature is the active principle that shapes, organizes, and governs all things according to rational law. When Marcus exhorts himself to live "according to Nature," he means living in harmony with this cosmic Reason, not simply "being natural" in any modern sense. Lowercase "nature" refers to individual character or the physical world in non-technical contexts.

Reason (*logos*, λόγος): Perhaps the most important concept in Stoic philosophy. *Logos* is simultaneously the rational structure of reality, God's intelligence, the law of Nature, Providence, and the human capacity to think rationally. These are not merely analogous but identical in Stoic thought. When capitalized, Reason refers to this cosmic principle; lowercase "reason" indicates ordinary thinking, arguments, or explanations.

God and the Gods (*theos*, θεός / *theoi*, θεοί): Stoicism is simultaneously monotheistic and polytheistic. There is one divine Reason pervading all things (God, singular), but Stoics also honored the traditional Olympian deities (the Gods, plural), understanding them as aspects or manifestations of the one divine Nature. Marcus freely uses both registers, and this translation preserves both without harmonizing.

Zeus (Ζεύς): For Stoics, essentially equivalent to God, Nature, cosmic Reason, and Fate. When Marcus addresses "O Zeus, O Nature," he treats these as different names for the same divine reality.

Cosmos (*kosmos*, κόσμος): The ordered universe; reality conceived as a rationally organized, living whole. The Greek word originally meant "order" or "ornament," and "Cosmos" preserves this emphasis on intelligent organization that "universe" or "world" would lack.

The Whole (*to holon*, τὸ ὅλον): The totality of reality conceived as an organic, unified living being, all parts working together as one system. Marcus frequently speaks of things benefiting or harming the Whole.

The All (*to pan*, τὸ πᾶν): The totality of everything that exists, emphasizing comprehensive totality rather than organic unity. The distinction from "the Whole" is subtle but occasionally significant.

Fate (*heimarmenē*, εἱμαρμένη): The unbreakable chain of causes that determines all events. Stoic Fate is not blind, arbitrary, or meaningless. It is identical with Providence, Nature, and Reason. What happens by Fate happens according to divine Reason.

Providence (*pronoia*, πρόνοια): Divine forethought and care; the rational governance of the Cosmos by God. Marcus repeatedly poses the question "Atoms or Providence?", the fundamental choice between Epicurean materialism and Stoic teleology. He consistently affirms Providence.

present perceived good. **Distress** (*lypē*, λύπη) is irrational contraction at a present perceived evil. Each generic Passion has numerous subspecies: Anger is a species of Desire, Envy a species of Distress, and so on.

The sage achieves Apatheia, complete freedom from these four Passions, and instead experiences three rational **Good Emotions** (*eupatheiai*, εὐπάθειαι): **Joy** (*chara*, χαρά), the rational counterpart to Pleasure; **Wish** (*boulēsis*, βούλησις), the rational counterpart to Desire; and **Caution** (*eulabeia*, εὐλάβεια), the rational counterpart to Fear. There is no rational counterpart to Distress, because the sage recognizes that nothing truly evil is ever present.

These terms are capitalized when Marcus uses them in their technical Stoic sense and left lowercase when the context is clearly non-technical.

Value Theory

Virtue (*aretē*, ἀρετή): Excellence of character; living according to Nature and Reason. For Stoics, Virtue is the only true Good, and it alone suffices for Flourishing. The cardinal Virtues are **Wisdom** (*sophia*, σοφία) or **Practical Wisdom** (*phronēsis*, φρόνησις), **Justice** (*dikaiosynē*, δικαιοσύνη), **Courage** (*andreia*, ἀνδρεία), and **Temperance** (*sōphrosynē*, σωφροσύνη).

Vice (*kakia*, κακία): The opposite of Virtue; the only true Evil in Stoic ethics.

The Good (*to agathon*, τὸ ἀγαθόν): In Stoic ethics, only Virtue qualifies. Nothing external (wealth, health, reputation, life itself) is truly Good.

Indifferents (*adiaphora*, ἀδιάφορα): Everything that is neither Virtue nor Vice: health, wealth, reputation, pain, pleasure, life, and death. These are subdivided into **Preferred Indifferents** (*proēgmena*), things that accord with Nature and are worth selecting though not truly Good, and **Dispreferred Indifferents** (*apoproēgmena*), things contrary to Nature and worth avoiding though not truly Evil.

Flourishing (*eudaimonia*, εὐδαιμονία): The fulfilled human life; living well. English "happiness" suggests pleasant feelings; Stoic Flourishing is objective human excellence, living according to Virtue, which may or may not feel pleasant. The word literally means "having a good *daimōn*."

The Physical World

Matter (*hylē*, ὕλη): The passive principle in Stoic physics, shaped and organized by Reason. Reality consists of two principles: active (Reason, God, Pneuma) and passive (Matter). Together they constitute the living Cosmos.

Void (*kenon*, κενόν): Empty space. Stoics held that the Cosmos contains no Void. It is fully filled with Matter and Pneuma. Void exists only outside the Cosmos, surrounding it infinitely.

Atoms (*atomoi*, ἄτομοι): Indivisible particles of matter according to Epicurean physics. "Atoms or Providence" represents the choice between Epicurean materialism and Stoic teleology, not a statement about Atoms producing anything.

Body (*sōma*, σῶμα): Any corporeal thing. For Stoics, only bodies are fully real; only bodies can act or be acted upon. This includes Psyche, Reason, God, and Pneuma, all corporeal. Capitalized in philosophical contexts; lowercase for ordinary bodily references.

Change and Dissolution

Among Marcus's most persistent themes: **Transformation** (*metabolē*, μεταβολή), the constant flux of all things, of one thing becoming another, **Transition** (*metastasis*, μετάστασις), the movement from one state to another, or a shift in position, **Generation** (*genesis*, γένεσις), **Decay/Destruction** (*phthor*, φθορά), and **Dissolution** (*dialysis*, διάλυσις) are the complementary processes of coming-into-being and passing-away. All are natural, all the work of Nature, none to be feared. Capitalized in philosophical contexts; lowercase in ordinary descriptive usage.

Ethical Action

Appropriate Action (*kathēkon*, καθῆκον): Actions befitting a rational being; "duties" in the broad sense. Performed by both sages and non-sages. Distinct from **Right Action** (*katorthōma*, κατόρθωμα), which is an Appropriate Action performed with perfect Virtue and complete understanding. Only the sage performs Right Actions.

Reservation (*hypexhairesis*, ὑπεξαίρεσις): Acting with the mental reservation "if nothing prevents it" or "if Fate allows." The Stoic practice of pursuing goals while accepting that outcomes are not in our power. It prevents attachment to outcomes while permitting vigorous action.

Social and Political Life

Community or **Fellowship** (*koinōnia*, κοινωνία): The bond among Rational beings. Marcus emphasizes this heavily: we exist for one another. The concept extends to the cosmic Community of all rational beings under common Reason.

Commonwealth (*politeia*, πολιτεία): The organized political community, extended by Marcus to the cosmic Commonwealth of all Rational beings living under common Reason.

Time and Causation

Eternity (*aiōn*, αἰών): Vast cosmic time; the immense duration against which individual human lives shrink to nothing.

The Present (*to nyn*, τὸ νῦν): The now; the only time in which we actually live. The past is gone, the future uncertain. Stoic Practice focuses attention on present action.

Cause (*aitia*, αἰτία): That which brings about an effect. "The Causal" refers to the active, form-giving aspect of explanation, as opposed to the Material.

Necessity (*anankē*, ἀνάγκη): What must be; causal inevitability; the necessary character of Fate's unfolding.

Chance or **Fortune** (*tychē*, τύχη): What appears random. Stoics deny ultimate randomness; apparent Chance results from causes we cannot trace.

Practice and Attention

Practice or **Training** (*askēsis*, ἄσκησις): Philosophical exercise; disciplined training of the Psyche. Not primarily physical austerity but any practice that shapes the Psyche toward Virtue.

Attention or **Vigilance** (*prosochē*, προσοχή): Mindful watchfulness over one's Judgments and Impressions; the sustained effort required to live philosophically.

Analysis (*analysis*, ἀνάλυσις): Breaking things down to their constituent parts. Marcus's characteristic technique of stripping away appearances and Impressions to reveal bare reality. Used for decomposing events into Matter and Cause, or reducing impressive-seeming things to their physical elements.

3. Key Phrases

"According to Nature" (*kata physin*, κατὰ φύσιν): Living in harmony with cosmic Reason: accepting Fate, fulfilling social roles, cultivating Virtue, acting rationally.

"Contrary to Nature" (*para physin*, παρὰ φύσιν): What violates rational order; Vice; the Passions that represent the Psyche in rebellion against Reason.

"Up to us" (*eph' hēmin*, ἐφ' ἡμῖν): The Stoic dichotomy of control. Only Judgments, Assent, Impulses, and choices are truly ours; everything external lies outside our control. Freedom comes from recognizing this.

"Atoms or Providence" (*atomoi ē pronoia*, ἄτομοι ἢ πρόνοια): The fundamental choice between worldviews. Either reality is random atomic collision (Epicureanism) or rational divine order (Stoicism). Marcus consistently affirms Providence.

"Common Nature" (*hē koinē physis*, ἡ κοινὴ φύσις): Universal Nature as shared by all rational beings.

"Common Reason" (*koinos logos,* κοινὸς λόγος): The universal Reason in which all rational beings participate; the basis for natural law and human Community.

4. On Stoic Materialism

A word of philosophical orientation may help readers unfamiliar with ancient Stoicism.

Modern readers often assume that "spiritual" and "material" are opposites, that God, souls, and minds must be immaterial to be real or valuable. The Stoics held precisely the opposite view. For them, only bodies are fully real, because only bodies can act or be acted upon. Anything that makes a difference in the world must be corporeal.

This means that Stoic God, Psyche, Reason, and Virtue are all material, composed of Pneuma, the refined fiery air that pervades and animates all things. This is not a demotion but an affirmation: these realities are causally efficacious, genuinely present in the physical world, not relegated to some separate immaterial realm.

Four things exist incorporeally in Stoic thought: time, Void, place, and *lekta* (sayables or meanings). But precisely because they are incorporeal, they cannot act or be acted upon. They are, in a sense, less real than bodies.

This materialism has ethical implications. We are not immortal "souls" temporarily housed in bodies, awaiting release to a better world. We are embodied rational animals whose Psyches may well disperse at death. This makes present life and present Virtue all the more urgent. There may be nothing beyond.

5. On the Identity of Divine Concepts

One of Stoicism's most distinctive doctrines is the identification of concepts that seem, to modern readers, obviously distinct:

Nature = God = Reason = Providence = Fate = Zeus

These are not different entities but different names for the same reality:

the rational principle that orders the Cosmos. Nature is God considered as the source of growth and life. Providence is God considered as caring for creation. Fate is God considered as the necessary sequence of causes. Reason is God considered as intelligence. Zeus is God considered under traditional religious names.

When Marcus prays to Zeus, philosophizes about Nature, accepts Fate, trusts Providence, or follows Reason, he is relating to the same divine reality under different descriptions. This translation preserves his varied vocabulary without artificially harmonizing it, allowing readers to see both the underlying unity and the different emphases each term carries.

6. How This Translation Differs

George Long's 1862 translation, long the standard, is philosophically careful but uses Victorian English that now obscures meaning. Robin Hard's 2011 rendering is modern and literal but does not systematize its philosophical vocabulary. Gregory Hays's 2002 version is the most widely read today, brilliantly accessible but freely paraphrastic, often sacrificing precision for readability. C.R. Haines's 1916 Loeb edition is scholarly but conservative.

This translation attempts to combine the rigor of Long and Haines with the readability of Hays, while focusing on terminological consistency and philosophical precision.

The reader who approaches this translation will find Marcus Aurelius as he was: a tired, aging emperor writing to himself by lamplight on the Danubian frontier, trying to hold his own Psyche together through the discipline of Stoic Reason, preparing himself for a death he knew was coming, and finding in philosophy not comfort but clarity. That is what these notebooks offer, and that is what this translation attempts to preserve.

Works Cited

Source Texts (Greek Editions)

Marcus Aurelius. *M. Antonini Imperatoris Romani, et Philosophi, De seipso seu vita sua Libri XII*. Graecè & Latinè nunc primùm editi. Translated by Wilhelm Xylander. Tiguri [Zürich]: Apud Andream Gesnerum F., 1558/59. *Editio princeps*, based on the now-lost *Codex Palatinus* (P; also designated *Codex Toxitanus*, T). This volume also contains: Xylander's Latin translation; Xylander's Dedicatory Epistle (Latin); Conrad Gessner's Dedicatory Epistle (Greek); excerpts from the Suda on Marcus Aurelius (Greek and Latin); excerpts from Sextus Aurelius Victor, *Epitome de Caesaribus*; and Marinus of Neapolis, *De Procli Vita et Foelicitate*.

Marcus Aurelius. *M. Antoninus Imperator Ad Se Ipsum*. Edited by I. H. Leopold. Oxford Classical Texts. Oxford: Clarendon Press, 1908. Used throughout as the Modern Greek comparison text.

Primary Sources: Ancient Texts

Aeschylus. *Danaides*, Fr. 44 Nauck. In August Nauck, ed., *Tragicorum Graecorum Fragmenta*. 2nd ed. Leipzig: Teubner, 1889.

Democritus. Fr. B9 Diels-Kranz. In Hermann Diels and Walther Kranz, eds., *Die Fragmente der Vorsokratiker*. 6th ed. Berlin: Weidmann, 1951-1952.

Diogenes Laertius. *Lives of the Eminent Philosophers*. Translated by R. D. Hicks. Loeb Classical Library. 2 vols. Cambridge, MA: Harvard University Press, 1925.

Empedocles. Fragments (Diels-Kranz). In Hermann Diels and Walther Kranz, eds., *Die Fragmente der Vorsokratiker*. 6th ed. Berlin: Weidmann, 1951-1952.

Epictetus. *Dissertationes ab Arriano Digestae* [*Discourses*]. Edited by Heinrich

Schenkl. 2nd ed. Leipzig: Teubner, 1916.

Epictetus. *Enchiridion*. Edited by Heinrich Schenkl. 2nd ed. Leipzig: Teubner, 1916.

Epicurus. Fr. 447 Usener. In Hermann Usener, ed., *Epicurea*. Leipzig: Teubner, 1887.

Euripides. *Antiope*, Fr. 208 Kannicht. In Richard Kannicht, ed., *Tragicorum Graecorum Fragmenta*. Vol. 5. Göttingen: Vandenhoeck & Ruprecht, 2004.

Euripides. *Bellerophon*, Fr. 286 Nauck. In August Nauck, ed., *Tragicorum Graecorum Fragmenta*. 2nd ed. Leipzig: Teubner, 1889.

Euripides. *Chrysippus*, Fr. 839 Nauck. In August Nauck, ed., *Tragicorum Graecorum Fragmenta*. 2nd ed. Leipzig: Teubner, 1889.

Euripides. *Hypsipyle*, Fr. 757 Nauck. In August Nauck, ed., *Tragicorum Graecorum Fragmenta*. 2nd ed. Leipzig: Teubner, 1889.

Euripides. *Suppliants*.

Euripides. Fr. 898 Nauck. In August Nauck, ed., *Tragicorum Graecorum Fragmenta*. 2nd ed. Leipzig: Teubner, 1889.

Gessner, Conrad. Dedicatory Epistle (Greek). In Xylander, *M. Antonini Imperatoris*. Zürich, 1558/59. English translation included in back matter of the present volume.

Heraclitus. Fragments (Diels-Kranz). In Hermann Diels and Walther Kranz, eds., *Die Fragmente der Vorsokratiker*. 6th ed. Berlin: Weidmann, 1951-1952.

Herodotus. *Histories*.

Hesiod. *Works and Days*.

Homer. *Iliad*.

Homer. *Odyssey*.

Horace. *Ars Poetica*.

Horace. *Satires*.

Iamblichus. *De Vita Pythagorica*.

Menander. *Phasma* [*The Apparition*], lines 17-18.

Plato. *Apology, Gorgias, Phaedo, Republic, Sophist, Theaetetus*. In John Burnet, ed., *Platonis Opera*. Oxford: Clarendon Press, 1900-1907.

Sextus Aurelius Victor. *Epitome de Caesaribus* (excerpts on Marcus

Aurelius). As reproduced in Xylander, *M. Antonini Imperatoris.* Zürich, 1558/59. English translation included in back matter of the present volume.

Sophocles. *Oedipus Tyrannus.*

Suda (excerpts on Marcus Aurelius). As reproduced in Xylander, *M. Antonini Imperatoris.* Zürich, 1558/59. Critical edition: Ada Adler, ed., *Suidae Lexicon.* 5 vols. Leipzig: Teubner, 1928-1938. English translation included in back matter of the present volume.

Xylander, Wilhelm. Dedicatory Epistle (Latin). In Xylander, *M. Antonini Imperatoris.* Zürich, 1558/59. English translation included in back matter of the present volume.

Ancient Sources Cited in Footnotes

Cicero. *Tusculan Disputations.*

Historia Augusta. Translated by David Magie. Loeb Classical Library. 3 vols. Cambridge, MA: Harvard University Press, 1921-1932.

Lucian. *Imagines.*

Modern Translations of Marcus Aurelius's *Meditations*

Farquharson, A. S. L. *The Meditations of the Emperor Marcus Antoninus.* Edited with translation and commentary. 2 vols. Oxford: Clarendon Press, 1944.

Haines, C. R. *Marcus Aurelius.* Loeb Classical Library 58. Cambridge, MA: Harvard University Press, 1916.

Hard, Robin. *Marcus Aurelius: Meditations, with Selected Correspondence.* Oxford World's Classics. Oxford: Oxford University Press, 2011.

Hays, Gregory. *Meditations: A New Translation.* New York: Modern Library, 2002.

Long, George. *The Thoughts of the Emperor M. Aurelius Antoninus.* London: Bell and Daldy, 1862.

Secondary Sources

Arnott, W. G., ed. and trans. *Menander.* Vol. 3. Loeb Classical Library 460. Cambridge, MA: Harvard University Press, 2000.

Pyle, C. M. "Conrad Gessner on the Spelling of His Name." *Archives of Natural History* 27, no. 2 (2000): 175-186.

Notes

ON THE XYLANDER TEXTS

1   Andreas Gessner was Conrad Gessner's cousin and the printer who produced the 1558/59
    editio princeps in Zurich. The title page of the edition reads *Apud Andream Gesnerum
    F.* ("at the press of Andreas Gesner the Younger"). The spelling of the family name has
    been a source of scholarly confusion for over 250 years. Both Conrad and Andreas
    published under the Latinized form *Gesnerus*, which lacks the double-s, and Conrad's
    Greek dedicatory epistle Hellenizes it as Γεσνῆρος (*Gesnēros*). However, in German, Conrad
    consistently signed his surname "Geßner" or "Gessner." The single-s "Gesner" is an
    incorrect back-formation from the Latin. See C.M. Pyle, "Conrad Gessner on the Spelling
    of His Name," *Archives of Natural History* 27.2 (2000), 175-186. The Library of Congress
    updated its authority record accordingly. This edition uses the correct German vernacular
    spelling "Gessner" for both cousins.

2   George Long, *The Meditations of Marcus Aurelius Antoninus* (London: Bell and Daldy, 1862),
    commentary on Book 1.

BOOK 1

3   Marcus Annius Verus (c. 50-138 CE), Marcus Aurelius's paternal grandfather, was a
    wealthy and politically prominent Roman who served three times as consul. He raised
    Marcus after his father's early death.

4   Marcus Annius Verus, Marcus Aurelius's biological father, who died when Marcus was
    approximately three years old. He served as praetor.

5   Domitia Lucilla (Minor), a wealthy Roman noblewoman who was known for her Greek
    learning. She remained influential in Marcus's life until her death around 155-161 CE.

6   Likely Lucius Catilius Severus, Marcus's maternal great-grandfather, who served as consul
    twice (110 and 120 CE) and was prefect of Rome.

7   The Greek *tropheus* (τροφεύς), "rearer" or "nurturer," denotes the adult male in an elite
    Roman household responsible for a child's overall upbringing and moral formation,
    distinct from academic tutors. This figure was typically a trusted slave or freedman.
    His name is not recorded in any surviving source. The practical virtues Marcus attributes
    to him suggest a man of old-fashioned character who shaped Marcus's disposition before
    Philosophy entered the picture.

8   There were four chariot-racing factions in Rome, each identified by color: the Reds

(*Russati*), Whites (*Albati*), Blues (*Veneti*), and Greens (*Prasini*). Marcus names only the Greens and Blues.

9   The Parmularii and Scutarii were the two great supporter factions of the gladiatorial arena, parallel to the chariot-racing factions mentioned just before. The Parmularii backed gladiators who carried a small shield (*parmula*), most notably the Thracians; the Scutarii backed those who carried the large legionary shield (*scutum*), most notably the Murmillones. Like the Blues and Greens of the circus, these rivalries organized Roman popular enthusiasm into fiercely partisan camps.

10   Diognetus was Marcus's painting teacher who also introduced him to Philosophy. His influence in turning Marcus away from superstition and toward philosophical inquiry was foundational.

11   In Ancient Rome, quail fighting was a mania similar to modern cockfighting, but often considered even more obsessive. Young aristocrats would carry quails in their robes and bet huge sums on their aggression.

12   These were early philosophical teachers of Marcus. Baccheius was likely a Platonist teacher. Tandasis and Marcianus are otherwise unknown but were evidently Marcus's first exposures to philosophical dialogue.

13   The "Greek training" (*Hellēnikē agōgē*) refers to the austere lifestyle associated with philosophical discipline: simple bedding, plain food, and physical hardship. This was inspired by Spartan and Cynic practices adopted by Stoics.

14   Quintus Junius Rusticus (c. 100-170 CE), a distinguished Stoic philosopher who served as *suffect* consul in 133 and *ordinary* consul in 162. He served as urban prefect from 162-168.

15   The Xylander text prints εὐεργετικόν (*euergetikon*, "benefactor") where modern critical editions read ἐνεργητικόν (*energētikon*, "man of action"). The Xylander reading pairs with ἀσκητικόν ("ascetic"): Marcus learned not to parade either his self-denial or his generosity. The modern reading shifts the warning to performative industriousness. This translation follows Xylander.

16   Sinuessa was a Roman coastal town in Campania (modern Mondragone, Italy), known as a resort destination.

17   Xylander reads εὐδιαλέκτως (*eudialektōs*, "easy to speak with") where modern editions have εὐδιαλλάκτως (*eudiallaktōs*, "easily reconciled").

18   Epictetus (c. 50/55-135 CE) was a former slave who became one of the most influential Stoic philosophers. His teachings, preserved in the *Discourses* and the *Enchiridion* (Handbook), profoundly shaped Marcus's thought.

19   Apollonius of Chalcedon, a Stoic philosopher whom Antoninus Pius summoned to Rome specifically to teach Marcus.

20   Sextus of Chaeronea, a philosopher and grandson of Plutarch.

21   Alexander of Cotiaeum (in Phrygia), Marcus's Greek grammar teacher. He was highly

respected and Marcus later appointed him to a secretarial position. Not to be confused with Alexander the Platonist (1.12).

22   Xylander reads ἀρκέσεως (*arkeseōs*, "sufficiency/furnishing what is adequate") where modern critical editions read ἀποκρίσεως (*apokriseōs*, "reply/answer"). Xylander reading suggests that the correction is delivered not as a direct response but by simply supplying what was needed, modeling correct usage without drawing attention to the error. This translation follows Xylander.

23   Xylander reads ὑπομνήσεως (*hypomnēseōs*, "reminder") where modern editions read παρυπομνήσεως (*parypomnēseōs*, "indirect reminder"). The Xylander reading is more straightforward. This translation follows Xylander.

24   Marcus Cornelius Fronto (c. 100-166 CE), the most famous Latin orator of his age, who served as Marcus's rhetoric teacher.

25   Alexander of Seleucia, also known as Alexander Peloplaton ("Clay-Plato"), was a Platonist philosopher who served as Marcus's Greek secretary.

26   Cinna Catulus, a Stoic philosopher.

27   Domitius is likely Gnaeus Domitius Afer (d. 59 CE), the famous orator. Athenodotus was a Stoic philosopher, pupil of Musonius Rufus, and teacher of Fronto (Marcus's rhetoric tutor).

28   Gnaeus Claudius Severus Arabianus (consul 146 CE), a Peripatetic philosopher. His son married one of Marcus's daughters.

29   These are five exemplars of principled resistance to tyranny, most of them Stoics. Thrasea Paetus (d. 66 CE) was a Roman senator condemned to death by Nero. Helvidius Priscus (d. c. 75 CE) was Thrasea's son-in-law, executed by Vespasian for his outspoken republican convictions. Cato (95-46 BCE), i.e. Cato the Younger (of Utica), the Stoic senator who killed himself rather than submit to Julius Caesar's dictatorship. Dion (408-354 BCE) was a disciple of Plato who led a revolt against the tyrant Dionysius II of Syracuse. Brutus (85-42 BCE), i.e. Marcus Junius Brutus, the assassin of Julius Caesar who killed himself after defeat at Philippi. All five are held up as men who chose death or ruin over submission to tyranny.

30   Maximus: Claudius Maximus, Stoic philosopher and suffect consul (c. 142 CE), one of Marcus's most important teachers. Marcus also mentions his death in 8.25.

31   Antoninus Pius (r. 138-161 CE), Marcus's adoptive father and predecessor as emperor. Marcus was adopted by Antoninus at Hadrian's direction in 138 CE.

32   "Passions for boys" (*erōtas tōn meirakiōn*): The Greek literally refers to the "erotic loves of lads/adolescents." Marcus lists it as a virtue that his father stopped this practice. Traditional translations often censor this to "he suppressed pederasty" or "he checked widespread vice." The raw translation is that he put an end to these specific erotic pursuits.

33   The Greek text actually uses a rare Latin loanword here: *Vernaculum* (βερνάχλον). A *vernaculus* was a "home-born slave," specifically the type known for being a "smart-aleck"

or a coarse jester.

34   "nor was he led astray by them": οὐδὲ μὴν εὐπαράγωγον ὑπ' αὐτῶν. This phrase is not present in the Xylander Greek text.

35   In Rome, bathing before the afternoon was considered a sign of idleness or debauchery. Bathing "out of time" (*aori*) meant you were slacking off.

36   Just as a rancher might count "heads" of cattle, Roman and Greek slave traders counted "bodies" (*somata*). In the context of the Roman slave market, *somata* (bodies) referred to human chattel. This exposes the dehumanizing reality of the time: the contemporary Roman attitude toward slaves as "bodies".

37   Xylander reads τελώνη (*telōnē*, "tax collector"): In modern critical Greek texts it reads φελώνη (*phelōnē*), which is a cloak or mantle (Latin: *paenula*). Since this passage deals primarily with simple clothing, "tax collector" in the original Xylander text may have been sourced from a damaged section of the original manuscript. One letter change alters the meaning of the entire passage. It seems odd that Marcus would be writing about simple clothing, and then bring up a random tax collector, when a single letter change would shift the meaning to "cloak", bringing the entire passage back onto topic. Here I attempted to preserve the Greek translation of the Xylander text as much as possible, even though the modern consensus seems to lean toward the cloak translation.

38   Lorium, Lanuvium, Tusculum: Imperial villas and towns near Rome where Antoninus Pius lived simply.
Lorium was an ancient village on the Via Aurelia, near modern Castel di Guido, approximately 19 km west of Rome. Antoninus Pius was raised here and died at his villa in 161 CE.
Lanuvium (modern Lanuvio) was an ancient city in the Alban Hills, approximately 32 km southeast of Rome. It was the ancestral home of the Antonine dynasty.
Tusculum was an ancient city near modern Frascati, approximately 25 km southeast of Rome. Famous for its patrician villas, it was destroyed in 1191 CE and never rebuilt.

39   Xylander translates to Latin as: ("His retinue from his estate was one who would escort him from the lower house: among the Lanuvians he generally made use of the Tusculan tax collector, even with [him] protesting.")

40   The section ends with a reference back to Maximus (1.15). This illness is mentioned again in 8.25.

41   Benedicta and Theodotus were possibly household slaves or freedpersons. Marcus is grateful to the Gods that he resisted sexual temptation toward members of his household.

42   Annia Galeria Faustina ("Faustina the Younger," c. 130-175 CE), Marcus Aurelius's cousin and wife, daughter of Antoninus Pius and Faustina the Elder.

43   Caieta (modern Gaeta, Italy) was a Roman port town on the coast of Latium, known as a resort area.

44   Some modern translations put "And how" or "So be it" or some other variation after this

sentence as a "fragment". In the original Xylander Greek text, this simply appears to be the first part of the next sentence on the next page.

45   The *"AMONG THE QUADI, BY THE GRANUA"* heading, along with sections 2.1 through 2.3, appear in both the Latin and Greek versions of Xylander in Book 1. The Book 2 heading of the Xylander texts starts with the modern section 2.4.

This heading is placed here, at the end of Book 1, to maintain accuracy with the Xylander texts. Many translations place it at the beginning of Book 2.

It is the translator's hypothesis that "Book 1", along with sections 2.1 through 2.3, was among the last passages of this work written.

The Granua (modern Hron River, Slovakia) flows through Quadi territory: where Marcus was campaigning in 179-180 CE.

Marcus died in March 180 at Vindobona (Vienna), never leaving this theater of war.

BOOK 2

46   τοῦτο ("this/it"): Refers to τὸ ἡγεμονικόν, the Ruling Faculty, which is the subject of the immediately preceding sentence. Marcus addresses himself: having dismissed the flesh as gore and bones, and the Pneuma as wind, he turns to the third and only essential component. The command is not to let the Ruling Faculty be enslaved any longer by unsociable Impulse, resentment of the present, or dread of the future.

47   Other modern consolidated Greek texts have θεουδῆ ("God-fearing") while Xylander has θεοειδῆ ("God-like"). Xylander translates to Latin as diuinae similem (= *divinae similem*) "similar/resembling the divine."

48   Theophrastus (Θεόφραστος, c. 371-287 BCE): Aristotle's closest colleague and successor as head of the Lyceum. A Peripatetic (Aristotelian) philosopher, not a Stoic, making Marcus's approving citation here notable.

49   Omitted in the Xylander Greek version.

50   "searches beneath the earth": Generally attributed to Pindar (c. 518-438 BCE), the Greek lyric poet. The expression describes someone who obsessively investigates hidden or unknowable things rather than attending to what is within their own power.

51   Daimon: Although defined in the front-matter glossary, this is the concept's first prominent appearance. Marcus's Daimon (δαίμων) is the divine rational element within each person, a fragment of the cosmic Logos.

52   Monimos the Cynic: Monimos (4th c. BCE): A Cynic philosopher from Syracuse. Famous for declaring 'everything is Opinion' (πᾶν ὑπόληψις). The saying resonates with the broader Cynic dismissal of conventional values as τῦφος ('smoke' or 'mist'). Marcus repurposes his Cynic skepticism for Stoic ends.

53   "the most ancient city and commonwealth": Not Rome, this refers to the Cosmos itself, understood in Stoic philosophy as a universal city-state (*cosmopolis*) governed by divine Reason (Logos), of which all rational beings are citizens. The foundation of Stoic cosmopolitanism.

BOOK 3

54   In the Xylander texts, this line exists in different books.

In the Greek edition, it is at the top of the page of the start of Book 3: Τὰ ἐν Καρνούντῳ. (*Ta en Karnountō*) "The [writings/things] in Carnuntum."
In the Latin edition, Xylander placed it as a footnote on the last page of Book 2: *Hæc Carnunti disputata.* ("These things were discussed at Carnuntum.")
Carnuntum was a major Roman legionary fortress and provincial capital on the Danube in Pannonia Superior, near modern Petronell-Carnuntum, Austria (~40 km east of Vienna).

55   Hippocrates: Hippocrates of Kos (c. 460-370 BCE): The most famous physician of antiquity, widely regarded as the "father of medicine."

56   The Chaldeans: In Greco-Roman usage, "Chaldean" had come to mean astrologer or fortune-teller, after the Babylonian priestly caste renowned for their astronomical and divinatory expertise. Marcus's irony: those who predicted others' deaths could not foresee their own.

57   Alexander, Pompey, and Gaius Caesar: Alexander the Great (356-323 BCE), Gnaeus Pompeius Magnus (Pompey, 106-48 BCE), and Gaius Julius Caesar (100-44 BCE). Three of antiquity's greatest conquerors, all dead; Marcus groups them as examples of the futility of worldly power.

58   Heraclitus / Conflagration of the Cosmos: Heraclitus of Ephesus (c. 535-475 BCE): Pre-Socratic philosopher who taught that fire is the fundamental element and that the Cosmos undergoes periodic Conflagration. He died of dropsy (fluid accumulation) and attempted to cure himself by covering his body in cow dung, hoping the warmth would draw out the moisture. Marcus's irony is pointed: the philosopher of fire died waterlogged and dung-smeared.

59   "Lice destroyed Democritus, and other lice destroyed Socrates": The Greek word is *phtheires*, which means both "lice" (vermin) and, metaphorically, "destroyers/corrupters." For Democritus (c. 460-370 BCE), the atomist philosopher, though scholars note this tradition is more commonly associated with Pherecydes of Syros. For Socrates (c. 470-399 BCE), the "lice" are metaphorical, his accusers Meletus, Anytus, and Lycon, the petty men who brought him to trial and execution.

60   "vessel so much baser": Marcus calls the body a "vessel": a container for the Psyche. The imagery is Stoic: the body is a temporary housing, inferior to the Intellect and Daimon it serves.

61   "as Socrates said, withdrawn itself from the persuasions of sense": A reference to Socrates's arguments in Plato's *Phaedo* (64e-65a), where Socrates argues that the philosopher's Psyche withdraws as much as possible from the body and its senses in order to apprehend truth through Reason alone.

62   Xylander's Greek text reads τῷ λογικῷ καὶ ποιητικῷ ἀγαθῷ ("the Rational and Creative Good"), where modern critical editions read τῷ λογικῷ καὶ πολιτικῷ ἀγαθῷ ("the Rational

and Civic Good"). Xylander's Latin translation confirms his Greek reading: he renders the phrase as *bono ratione praedito, & effectrici* ("the good endowed with reason and productive power"). The modern reading is adopted here because πολιτικός is consistent with Marcus's repeated characterization of human beings as λογικὸν καὶ πολιτικὸν ζῷον ("Rational and Civic Animal"), a phrase that appears throughout the *Meditations* (e.g., 3.7, 6.44, 9.16). Notably, Xylander's own text reads πολιτικοῦ ζώου just lines later in 3.7, suggesting the variant arose from scribal confusion between the similar letter sequences πολιτικ- and ποιητικ-.

63   "that Supreme City, of which other cities are but households": Another reference to the Stoic cosmopolis. Here Marcus adds the striking image that all earthly cities, including Rome, are merely "households" within the greater city of the Cosmos.

64   "your own notebooks, nor the deeds of the ancient Romans and Greeks, nor the excerpts from writings": An autobiographical glimpse: Marcus reveals that he kept personal notebooks, read histories of Rome and Greece, and compiled excerpts from philosophical writings, a common elite Roman practice. He admonishes himself to stop accumulating knowledge and start living by it.

65   *Androgynoi* here does not mean "androgynous" in the modern sense. Other translators have translated this as "men who have made themselves into women".

66   Marcus lists the types of people that he considers are driven merely by "Impulse" (lust/desire/appetite) rather than Reason. He lists wild beasts, Phalaris (a tyrant who roasted people in a bronze bull), Nero (who murdered his own mother), and *androgynoi*.

67   Xylander reads θεὸς (*theos*, singular, "God") where modern critical editions read θεοὺς (*theous*, plural accusative, "Gods"). The singular could yield the reading "to whom God is not a guide" rather than "those who do not believe in the Gods." The plural is the standard Stoic usage, and Marcus consistently refers to "the Gods" throughout the *Meditations*. The modern reading is adopted here.

BOOK 4

68   "Either Providence or Atoms": Marcus's recurring disjunction: either divine Providence governs the Cosmos (Stoic view) or random atomic collision does (Epicurean view).

69   Xylander reads παρασκευῆς ("preparation"), where modern editions read κατασκευῆς ("constitution"). The modern reading is adopted here, as κατασκευή is the standard Stoic term for the natural Constitution of a rational being. The two words differ only by prefix and could be easily confused in manuscript transmission. Xylander's Greek also omits λύσις ("Dissolution") from the paired phrase, which the modern text supplies.

70   λύρα (lyra): "lyre" is present in Modern Greek texts, but omitted in the Xylander Greek text.

71   Traditionally attributed to Aristophanes, the Athenian comic playwright (c. 446-386 BCE).

72   Cecrops: Legendary first king of Athens; Marcus contrasts the narrow patriotism of Athenian civic identity with Stoic cosmopolitanism.

73 "without a tunic": An allusion to the Cynics, who rejected material possessions. Diogenes of Sinope was notorious for living with almost nothing.

74 Vespasian / Trajan: Vespasian (r. 69-79 CE), founder of the Flavian dynasty. Trajan (r. 98-117 CE), renowned expansionist emperor. Both recent enough to feel vivid, yet their worlds are entirely gone.

75 Modern translations and modern Greek sources have this name as Dentatus. Xylander's 1558/59 Greek copy records this name as *Leonnatus* (Λεοννάτος). Xylander's Latin translation also translates the name as Leonnatus. Leonnatus was selected because this translation is focused on the Xylander texts. It may be the result of corruption or scribal error, but is what is in both the Xylander Greek text and the Latin translation.

76 Camillus, Caeso, Volesus, Leonnatus; Scipio, Cato; Augustus, Hadrian, Antoninus. Camillus (c. 365 BCE): savior of Rome from the Gauls. Caeso: early Republican patrician. Volesus: an archaic Roman name. Scipio Africanus (d. 183 BCE): defeated Hannibal. Cato the Elder (d. 149 BCE): censor famed for severity. The last three are Marcus's imperial predecessors. Leonnatus (Λεοννάτος, 356-322 BCE) was a Macedonian officer of Alexander the Great. Modern editions read Dentatus (Manius Curius Dentatus, d. 270 BCE, hero of the Samnite Wars) where Xylander has Leonnatus; see footnote 73.

77 Clotho: One of the three Moirai (Fates). She spins the thread of human life; her sister Lachesis measures it and Atropos cuts it. Here a personification of destiny.

78 Epictetus: Stoic philosopher (c. 50-135 CE), born into slavery, whose *Discourses* and *Enchiridion* profoundly influenced Marcus.

79 Heraclitus fragments: Marcus strings together several sayings of Heraclitus (c. 535-475 BCE) on elemental transformation, forgetfulness, and wakefulness. The cycle earth → water → air → fire reflects his doctrine of perpetual flux.

80 Helike, Pompeii, Herculaneum: Three cities destroyed by natural catastrophe. Helike, a Greek city in Achaea, was submerged by earthquake and tsunami in 373 BCE. Pompeii and Herculaneum were buried by the eruption of Vesuvius in 79 CE.

81 "yesterday a drop of mucus, tomorrow pickled flesh or ashes": "Mucus" (or semen) = conception; "pickled flesh or ashes" = the two Roman treatments of the dead: embalming and cremation.

82 The named individuals, Cadicianus, Fabius, Julianus, Lepidus, are likely personal acquaintances of Marcus Aurelius. Their specific identities are uncertain.

BOOK 5

83 Asclepius: God of healing and medicine, son of Apollo. His temples (*Asclepieia*) served as healing centers throughout the ancient world.

84 An egg-white and sponge compress was a common treatment for eye infection. Marcus uses this to say: Philosophy should not be a lecture; it should be like a soothing balm for your infected eyes.

85   κιναίδου ἤ πόρνης ("of a catamite or a prostitute")

    kinaidou (κιναίδου): a catamite is the receptive male partner in sexual intercourse, particularly a boy or young man kept for sexual purposes. The term carried strong connotations of sexual passivity and social degradation in the Roman world. Most translations soften *kinaidos* to "effeminate person" or "pervert," which loses the specific sexual meaning of the Greek.

    pornēs (πόρνης): a prostitute.

    Marcus's point is philosophical: worldly possessions are so worthless that even the most degraded members of society, by Roman societal prejudices at the time, can possess them.

86   Standard Translations: "weakling," "effeminate person," or "childish."

    The Literal Meaning: It is the diminutive form of "woman." Marcus lists it alongside tyrants and beasts as a type of Psyche that has lost its Reason. He is afraid of his Psyche becoming petty, emotional, or irrational, traits he, in the context of Ancient Rome, culturally associated with women.

87   The Xylander text (1558, p. 52) reads a self-contained clause: "for it would fit under 'the good'." The joke fails because the listener has already categorized things under genuine Virtue. Modern critical editions emend ("the good") to ("the goods") and re-punctuate, making the words a quoted fragment from the lost comic line: "he could not hear the [phrase] 'on account of the goods.'"

88   "the comic poet": Menander (c. 342-290 BCE), *Phasma* (*The Apparition*), lines 17-18. The character Syros teases the wealthy young Pheidias: "As the saying goes, you're so well off you have nowhere to shit, I'd have you know!" Marcus cites it without naming the poet. The identification was established by W.G. Arnott in the Loeb Classical Library edition of Menander (Vol. III, 2000), noting that lines 17-18 of *Phasma* are "cited (without Menander's name) by Marcus Aurelius Antoninus 5.12." The surviving fragment also confirms that the phrase "on account of the goods" belongs to the comic line itself, supporting the modern critical reading of this passage over the Xylander text (see preceding note).

89   "Right Actions" (κατορθώσεις): The Stoic technical term *katorthōsis* (κατόρθωσις), meaning a perfectly correct action performed in accord with Reason.

90   "There is smoke, and I depart": A proverbial expression for leaving a place that has become intolerable. The Stoics held that suicide could be rational when circumstances make a virtuous life impossible, the "open door" doctrine (attributed to Epictetus).

91   "fled from the broad-wayed earth to Olympus": Adapted from Hesiod, *Works and Days* 197-200. In Hesiod, Aidōs (Reverence/Shame) and Nemesis (Righteous Indignation) depart the earth for Olympus at the end of the Iron Age. Marcus substitutes his own list, Trust, Reverence, Justice, Truth, to describe the moral desolation of human society.

92   "the old man" and the spinning top: The anecdote is obscure; possibly a reference to a Stoic or Cynic teacher who, on his deathbed, reminded his student that the prized objects of life are as trivial as a child's toy.

93 Xylander reads λαλῶν (*lalōn*, "prattling, chattering") where modern critical editions read καλῶν (*kalōn*, "calling out"). The words differ by a single initial letter. Xylander's reading gives the passage a sharper, more contemptuous tone: Marcus derides himself not merely for speaking from the platform but for idle babbling. This translation follows Xylander.

BOOK 6

94 Falernian wine: Falernian (*Falernum*) was the most prestigious and expensive wine in the Roman world, produced on the slopes of Mount Falernus in northern Campania.

95 "what Crates says about Xenocrates himself": Crates of Thebes (c. 365-285 BCE) was a Cynic philosopher; Xenocrates (c. 396-314 BCE) was head of Plato's Academy. The specific anecdote Marcus refers to does not survive elsewhere.

96 This text is frequently a target for softening or modification. Some translations omit it or translate to something similar to "management of a great estate."

97 A triple word reversal. Xylander reads **δυσφημεῖν** (slander/disparage) three times where Modern reads **εὐφημεῖν** (praise) three times. The prefix swaps δυσ- (bad) → εὐ- (good). Xylander's paradox: people restrain from *slandering* contemporaries but worry about *being slandered* by posterity. Modern's paradox: people refuse to *praise* the living but crave *being praised* by the unborn. The entire passage reverses. Translation follows Modern.

98 "Take care that you are not Caesarized": Marcus warns himself against the corrupting effects of imperial power: adopting the arrogance, cruelty, or self-indulgence associated with some of his predecessors.

99 "be as a disciple of Antoninus": Antoninus Pius (r. 138-161 CE), Marcus's adoptive father and predecessor as emperor.

100 Chrysippus, "the cheap and ridiculous verse": Chrysippus of Soli (c. 279-206 BCE), the head of the Stoic school, who systematized Stoic logic and physics.

101 The God of healing (Asclepius) doing the work of Demeter (the Goddess of agriculture).

102 Philistion, Phoebus, Origanion: Unknown individuals, possibly Marcus's personal acquaintances or recently deceased public figures.

103 Eudoxus, Hipparchus, Archimedes, Menippus: Eudoxus of Cnidus (c. 390-337 BCE): mathematician and astronomer. Hipparchus (c. 190-120 BCE): astronomer who cataloged the stars. Archimedes of Syracuse (c. 287-212 BCE): mathematician, physicist, and inventor. Menippus of Gadara (3rd c. BCE): Cynic philosopher known for satirical writings mocking human pretension.

BOOK 7

104 μέλος → μέρος : Changing one letter in Greek changes the meaning of the word from 'limb' to 'part'.

105 Democritus: A paraphrase of Democritus (c. 460-370 BCE), fr. B9.

106 Marcus here appropriates a characteristically Epicurean argument on pain, derived from

Epicurus (Fr. 447 Usener): pain that is unbearable carries you off quickly; pain that does not kill is bearable. The Stoics freely borrowed useful therapeutic arguments from rival schools when they served the practical goal of tranquility. See also 7.64, where Marcus cites "the saying of Epicurus" on the same theme.

107   Plato quotation: From Plato, *Republic* 486a. Socrates describes the philosophic Psyche as possessing "contemplation of all time and all Substance" to which human life appears small and death nothing fearful.

108   Attributed to Antisthenes.

109   Attributed to Euripides.

110   Euripides, *Antiope*, Fr. 208 (Kannicht). The reference to "two children" (dual form in Greek) alludes to Antiope's twin sons, Amphion and Zethus.

111   Socrates quotations: 7.44-45 quote Socrates from Plato's *Apology* (28b-d): a man of worth should not calculate the risk of death but only whether his actions are just. 7.46 draws from the *Gorgias* (512d-e): saving one's life is not the same as living nobly.

112   Plato, aerial view: Possibly adapted from Plato, *Theaetetus* 174a-175b, or *Republic* 500b-c. The philosopher surveys human affairs from above, a common Platonic and Stoic exercise for gaining detachment.

113   Euripides quotation: From Euripides, *Chrysippus* (fr. 839). Famous in antiquity; translated by Lucretius and cited by Plutarch, Galen, and others. Expresses the cosmology of Anaxagoras: at death, the earthy returns to earth, the ethereal to the heavens. Marcus compares it against the Epicurean alternative.

114   The first two lines are from Euripides, *Suppliants* 1110-11. The second quotation ("a wind blowing from the Gods...") is of unknown authorship (fr. 303, *Tragicorum Graecorum Fragmenta*).

115   Attributed to Plato.

116   Epicurus: Epicurus, fr. 447 Usener. A notable instance of Marcus borrowing from a rival school's founder for practical use.

117   Telauges was reputedly the son of Pythagoras and Theano. Almost nothing is known of him from independent sources; our primary testimony comes from Iamblichus, *De Vita Pythagorica*. Marcus's provocative question, whether an obscure Pythagorean might have possessed a superior Psyche to Socrates, illustrates the Stoic principle that Virtue is internal and invisible, not measured by fame or eloquent death.

118   Socrates anecdotes: The incidents listed are well-attested: his noble death (*Phaedo*); enduring the frost at Potidaea (*Symposium* 220b-d); refusing to arrest Leon of Salamis under the Thirty Tyrants (*Apology* 32c-d); his alleged swagger (*Symposium* 221b).

BOOK 8

119   Alexander, Gaius, Pompey vs. Diogenes, Heraclitus, Socrates: Marcus contrasts three conquerors: Alexander the Great (356-323 BCE), Gaius Julius Caesar (100-44 BCE),

and Pompey the Great (106-48 BCE); with three philosophers: Diogenes of Sinope (c. 404-323 BCE), the Cynic; Heraclitus (c. 535-475 BCE); and Socrates (c. 470-399 BCE). The conquerors were enslaved to external cares; the philosophers' Ruling Faculties were self-sufficient.

120 "Lucilla buried Verus...": A litany of mourner-then-mourned pairs from Marcus's own family and the imperial court. Lucilla is Domitia Lucilla, Marcus's mother, who buried her husband M. Annius Verus (Marcus's father, who died c. 124 CE). Secunda is the wife of Claudius Maximus, Marcus's Stoic teacher (mentioned in 1.15). Epitynchanus and Diotimus are otherwise unknown, possibly imperial freedmen of the Antonine or Hadrianic households. Antoninus is Antoninus Pius (r. 138-161), who buried his wife Faustina the Elder (d. 140 CE). Celer is Caninius Celer, Hadrian's Greek secretary; the *Historia Augusta* confirms he "saw Hadrian to his grave and then went to his own."

121 Charax, Demetrius the Platonist, Eudaemon: Intellectuals of the preceding generation, now almost entirely forgotten, which is Marcus's point.

122 Almost all modern English editions translate this as "vessel" or "body". Xylander has this word as "αἴτιον" (cause). Xylander translates this to abbreviated Latin as "causam pximā" (i.e. causam proximam, "proximate cause").

123 Augustus (Gaius Octavius, later Gaius Julius Caesar Octavianus, 63 BCE-14 CE), the first Roman emperor (r. 27 BCE-14 CE).

124 Marcus Vipsanius Agrippa (c. 63-12 BCE), Augustus's closest friend, chief general, and son-in-law (married to Julia the Elder). He was the architect of Augustus's military victories, including the decisive naval battle of Actium (31 BCE).

125 "The Court of Augustus": Marcus surveys Augustus's entire household to show that even the most powerful dynasty is annihilated by time. Areius (Arius Didymus, d. after 9 BCE) was Augustus's personal philosopher. Maecenas (d. 8 BCE) was his great patron of the arts. "The Pompeys" refers to the extinction of Pompey the Great's family line.

126 Panthea of Smyrna was a celebrated beauty and the mistress of Lucius Verus, Marcus's co-emperor, during the Parthian campaign (162-166 CE). Marcus's phrasing implies she was still visiting the coffin years after Verus's death in 169 CE. She is described extensively in Lucian, Imagines, where she is praised as the most beautiful woman of the age. Marcus's question, "Do Panthea or Pergamus still sit by the tomb of Verus?", uses her as an example of the transience of even the most devoted attachments.
Pergamus is otherwise unknown, presumably a freedman or close attendant of Verus.

127 The Xylander text reads τοῦ Λυκίου σορῷ ("the coffin of Lucius"), where modern editions emend to Οὐήρου ("of Verus"). Both refer to the same man: Marcus's co-emperor and adoptive brother, Lucius Verus (130-169 CE). "Lucius" is the more intimate form and is adopted here from the Xylander reading.

128 Xylander prints Χαυρίας ("Chaurias"), possibly a typographical error for Χαβρίας (Chabrias), which is used by most modern translations.

129 "When it has become a sphere, it remains round": An allusion to the Stoic doctrine that the perfected mind is like a sphere: self-contained, offering no point of attack, rolling smoothly.

130 "The Mind, free from Passions, is a citadel": A celebrated metaphor. The Greek ἀκρόπολις ("citadel/acropolis") evokes both the literal Athenian Acropolis and the Stoic teaching that the Ruling Faculty is an inner fortress impervious to external assault.

BOOK 9

131 Xylander reads διαφοράς (*diaphoras*, "differences"), where modern critical editions read διαφθοράς (*diaphthoras*, "destructions"). The words differ by a single letter. The modern reading is adopted here as better suited to the passage's sustained imagery of cessation and death.

132 "You are a little Psyche carrying around a corpse": The Nekyia is Book 11 of Homer's Odyssey, where Odysseus summons and converses with the shades of the dead. The saying is attributed to Epictetus (see note on 4.41).

133 The Xylander Greek reads τὸ δὲ ὅλον, εἴ τις θεὸς οὐκ ἔχει ταῦτα ("if some god does not have these things"), a reading that is almost certainly corrupt, as it produces the opposite of Marcus's argument. The modern critical text reads εἴτε θεός, εὖ ἔχει πάντα ("whether God, all things are well"). Xylander himself appears to have recognized the corruption in his Greek manuscript, as his own Latin translation reads *siue Deus sit, recte omnia habent* ("whether God exists, all things are well"), following the sense of the modern text rather than his own Greek. This is one of the clearer instances where the Xylander Greek preserves a scribal error from the Palatine manuscript, and where Xylander's Latin serves as evidence that he had access to a better reading, whether by conjecture or from a source no longer extant. This translation follows Xylander's Latin.

134 "Do not hope for Plato's Republic": A famous concession to political realism. Plato's *Republic* describes an ideal city governed by philosopher-kings. Marcus, himself the closest historical approximation to a philosopher-king, admits the ideal is unattainable and counsels incremental progress instead.

135 Alexander, Philip, Demetrius of Phalerum: Alexander the Great (356-323 BCE) and his father Philip II of Macedon (382-336 BCE). Demetrius of Phalerum (c. 350-280 BCE) was a Peripatetic philosopher-statesman who governed Athens for ten years under Macedonian authority, later instrumental in founding the Library of Alexandria.

136 Note: Xylander reads τὸν ἴδιον αἰῶνα ("your own lifetime"); Modern Greek sources read τὸν ἀίδιον αἰῶνα ("everlasting Eternity"). The Xylander Greek reading is adopted here.

137 Xylander reads τὸ πνευματικὸν (*to pneumatikon*, "the pneumatic element"), an adjective treating the breath-component as a quality of Matter, where modern critical editions read τὸ πνευμάτιον (*to pneumation*, "the little Pneuma"), a diminutive noun characteristic of Marcus's self-deprecating style elsewhere (cf. σωμάτιον, "little body," and ὀστάρια, "little bones"). The modern reading is adopted here.

138 Xylander reads τὸ ἐνιαυτὸν ἔτεσι ('for a year'); Modern Greek sources read τὸ ἑκατὸν ἔτεσι ('for a hundred years'). The Xylander text is preserved here.

139 Epicurus in illness: Marcus paraphrases the deathbed conduct of Epicurus (341-270 BCE), founder of the rival Epicurean school. Epicurus's *Letter to Idomeneus*, written on his last day while suffering from the kidney stones and dysentery that would kill him, is preserved in Diogenes Laertius 10.22. Notable that Marcus cites an Epicurean exemplum approvingly; philosophical fortitude transcends philosophical school rivalry.

BOOK 10

140 The Xylander Greek text (1558, p. 118) reads φιλητικῆς καὶ στερητικῆς διαθέσεως (*philētikēs kai sterētikēs diatheseōs*), "the loving and depriving disposition," where στερητικῆς derives from στέρησις ("deprivation, wanting nothing"). Modern critical editions emend to στερκτικῆς (*sterktikēs*), from στέργω ("to love with natural affection"), yielding "the loving and affectionate disposition." The Xylander reading is preserved here: Marcus asks his Psyche whether it will ever attain the disposition that both loves and wants nothing, a reading reinforced by the lines that immediately follow ("full and without want, desiring nothing, yearning for nothing").

141 The Xylander text reads εἰς ἀλλοτρίωσιν ("alienation"), where modern editions emend to ἀλλοίωσιν ("alteration") to harmonize with ἀλλοιοῦσθαι two lines earlier. The Xylander reading is adopted here.

142 θηριομάχοι (beast-fighters): The *bestiarii* of the Roman arena: condemned criminals, prisoners of war, or professional fighters who faced wild animals. Marcus's use of ἡμιβρώτοις ("half-devoured") creates a shocking image of men literally being eaten alive yet begging for one more day.

143 This passage preserves Marcus's unvarnished view of arena violence. The philosopher-emperor watched such spectacles (as duty required) but here uses them as a metaphor for the unphilosophical life: clinging to existence while being destroyed by Passions and circumstance.

144 "Islands of the Blessed": In Greek mythology, the Isles of the Blessed (μακάρων νῆσοι) were a paradise at the edge of the world where heroes and the virtuous dwelt after death.

145 Sarmatians: An Iranian nomadic people on the Danubian frontier whom Marcus fought during the Marcomannic Wars (c. 166-180 CE).

146 This fragment is attributed to Euripides (Fr. 898 Nauck), but an older scholarly tradition assigns closely related lines to Aeschylus's lost Danaides (Fr. 44 Nauck). Both fragments describe the cosmic eros between Earth and Sky: rain as the desire of Aether to penetrate the Earth, and Earth's reciprocal longing. The attribution remains disputed; Marcus quotes the lines without naming their author.

147 Plato, "enclosing a fold on a mountain" / "milking his bleating flock": From Plato, *Theaetetus* 174d-e. Socrates says the true philosopher views a king or tyrant as merely a herdsman

penned up on a mountain, milking a troublesome animal. Marcus, himself the supreme ruler, ironically applies this anti-political image to his own situation.

148 δραπέτης (drapétēs): A runaway slave / fugitive slave. In the ancient Greek and Roman world, δραπέτης was a legal and social term for a slave who had fled from their master.

149 This sentence is often softened in other translations. The Greek is quite literal: Σπέρμα (Sperma): Seed, sperm, semen. εἰς (eis): Into, to. μήτραν (mētran): Womb, uterus. ἀφείς (apheis): Having released or sent forth. ἀπεχώρησε (apechōrēse): He withdrew.

150 "the power that makes things sink and rise": Greek has "τὴν βρίθουσαν καὶ τὴν ἀνωφερῆ" literally "the weighing-down [force] and the upward-bearing [force]." In ancient physics (Aristotelian and Stoic), these were two distinct natural tendencies: heavy elements (earth, water) move downward toward the cosmic center, while light elements (fire, air) move upward.

151 Philip, Alexander, Croesus: Philip II of Macedon (382-336 BCE), father of Alexander the Great. Croesus (c. 595-546 BCE), last king of Lydia, proverbial for wealth and catastrophic reversal of fortune (Herodotus 1.30-86). All paired with the Roman imperial courts of Hadrian and Antoninus Pius to show identical patterns across civilizations.

152 Σωκρατικός (Socraticus): A personal name meaning "follower of Socrates" or "Socratic one," not the philosopher Socrates himself. One of Marcus's contemporaries who has since died.

153 Satyron, Euphrates, Alciphron, Xenophon, etc.: A list pairing Marcus's contemporaries with their predecessors, now dead. The only externally known figure is Euphrates the Stoic philosopher (c. 35-118 CE), praised by Pliny and Epictetus. The others are Marcus's acquaintances, otherwise unknown, which is the point.

154 "Leaves: some the wind pours down to the ground": Homer, *Iliad* 6.146-149. Glaucus to Diomedes: "As the generation of leaves, so is that of men."

155 The Xylander Greek text (1558, p. 131) reads δύσποτμος (*dyspotmos*, "unfortunate/ill-fated"), while modern critical Greek editions read εὔποτμος (*eupotmos*, "fortunate"). Curiously, Xylander's own Latin translation (p. 169) renders the passage as *"Nemo est adeò felix"* ("No one is so fortunate"), directly contradicting his printed Greek. This discrepancy raises the possibility of a typesetting error in the Greek edition that did not carry over into the Latin, which may have been typeset independently or from a separate manuscript. The Greek and Latin editions of Xylander's 1558/59 publication were printed as companion volumes, and a compositor unfamiliar with Greek could easily confuse the prefixes δύσ- and εὔ-, a single-letter difference that reverses the meaning entirely. The rhetorical logic favors "fortunate": Marcus's point is that even the most blessed person will have detractors at his deathbed. That Xylander's Latin agrees with modern editions suggests he understood the intended reading to be εὔποτμος, regardless of what appeared in his printed Greek. The corrected Xylander Latin reading is preserved here instead of the Xylander Greek.

BOOK 11

156 Pancratium (παγκράτιον): An ancient Greek combat sport combining wrestling and boxing, with virtually no restrictions except biting and eye-gouging.

157 A reference to the early Christians who were being actively persecuted by the Roman Empire at the time.

158 "Alas, Cithaeron!": Sophocles, *Oedipus Tyrannus* 1391. Oedipus's lament upon learning he was exposed on this mountain as an infant. Marcus's point: even the most anguished still endure their fate.

159 Euripides, *Antiope*, Fr. 208 (Kannicht). The reference to "two children" (dual form in Greek) alludes to Antiope's twin sons, Amphion and Zethus. Note: Some older commentaries may conflate this with the *Bellerophon* fragments quoted immediately adjacent to it in Book 7. Also quoted by Marcus in 7.41.

160 Euripides (from an unidentified lost play). The full line reads "For one must not rage against circumstances; they care nothing for it." Marcus quotes only the first half.

161 Euripides, *Hypsipyle:* The seer Amphiaraus consoles the grieving Hypsipyle after the death of the infant Opheltes: "It is our inevitable lot to reap life like a fruitful ear of grain, for one to live, and another not." Marcus also quotes this line at 7.40.

162 Old Comedy, Middle Comedy, New Comedy / Diogenes: Marcus traces the history of Athenian drama as a history of declining philosophical utility. Old Comedy (Aristophanes, c. 446-386 BCE) used παρρησία, frank, abrasive public speech, to combat pomposity. Diogenes the Cynic (c. 404-323 BCE) used similar shock tactics. Middle Comedy (c. 400-320 BCE) lost this edge; New Comedy (Menander, c. 342-290 BCE) devolved into polished entertainment.

163 Phocion (Φωκίων, c. 402-318 BCE) was an Athenian statesman and general who became legendary for his incorruptibility, austere virtue, and imperturbable calm: qualities that made him a natural exemplar for Stoic writers. When unjustly condemned to death, he told his son to bear no grudge against the Athenians.

164 Smells of goat: Greek *grasōn:* the pungent, unmistakable musk of a billy goat. Marcus's point: genuine character, like goat-stench, announces itself without words.

165 Apatheia: Greek ἀπάθεια, freedom from destructive Passions through correct judgment; not emotionlessness, but rational equanimity. Marcus's point: this is true power; anger and grief signal weakness.

166 Leader of the Muses: Greek *Mousēgetēs*, an epithet of Apollo, god of music, poetry, and rational enlightenment. Having presented nine precepts as "gifts from the Muses," Marcus playfully offers a tenth from their divine chief.

167 Xylander reads ὀλίγον γε βίαιον (*oligon ge biaion*, "little compulsion") where modern critical editions read οὐδέν γε βίαιον (*ouden ge biaion*, "nothing violent"). Modern editions deny any compulsion on the Intellectual part; Xylander concedes a slight compulsion, making the rational faculty's disobedience all the more inexcusable. This translation follows Xylander.

168 Xylander omits τὰς ὀργάς (*tas orgas*, "anger") from this list of departures from Nature. Xylander's text lists four: injustice, intemperance, Distress, and Fear. Modern critical editions add anger, producing five.

169 Xylander reads ἰσότητα (*isotēta*, "equality" or "equity") where modern critical editions read ὁσιότητα (*hosiotēta*, "sanctity" or "holiness"). The two words differ by a single letter and are easily confused in manuscript transmission. Modern editions also read εὐκοινωνησίας (*eukoinōnēsias*, "good fellowship") where Xylander has κοινωνησίας (*koinōnēsias*, "fellowship") without the εὐ- prefix. This translation follows Xylander in both cases.

170 "The country mouse and the city mouse": Allusion to the famous Aesopic fable (Perry 352), best known from Horace, *Satires* 2.6.79-117, where a country mouse, terrified by the dangers of luxurious urban life, flees back to his woodland hole.

171 The Lamia (Λάμια) was a mythological monster: a child-devouring bogeywoman used by Greek nurses to frighten children into obedience. Socrates's point: the opinions of the masses are like these nursery terrors, frightening only to the childish and philosophically immature.

172 Lacedaemonians: The Spartans, renowned for austere self-discipline. They provided comfort for others while disdaining it for themselves.

173 Socrates and Perdiccas: Marcus names Perdiccas, but the better-attested tradition (Diogenes Laertius 2.25) says Socrates refused the invitation of Archelaus, king of Macedon (r. 413-399 BCE), son and successor of Perdiccas II. Socrates declined because accepting royal hospitality he could not reciprocate would place him in a position of moral debt, a form of subjection he considered shameful.

174 Ephesians: Xylander has "Ephesians" in both Greek and Latin texts. Some manuscripts read "Epicureans" (Ἐπικουρείων), which would attribute this precept to the Epicurean school, known for meditating on exemplary sages. "Ephesians" may refer to writings associated with Ephesus, possibly Heraclitean traditions.

175 Pythagoreans / looking at the sky at dawn: The Pythagorean practice of morning sky-gazing is attested in several ancient sources (Iamblichus, *De Vita Pythagorica* 256; Diogenes Laertius 8.17). The stars' regularity, purity, and "nakedness" (they have nothing to conceal) serve as models for philosophical life.

176 Xanthippe (Ξανθίππη, Xanthippē) was the wife of Socrates, and her name became proverbial in antiquity for a shrewish, difficult, or quarrelsome spouse.

177 Euripides. The specific play from which the line derives is lost.

178 Homer, *Odyssey* 9.413.

179 Hesiod, *Works and Days* 190-194, from the Iron Age prophecy (174-201). Hesiod foretells a degenerate era when "there will be no favor for the man who keeps his oath or for the just or for the good; but rather men will praise the evil-doer."

180 A famous teaching of Epictetus (cf. *Discourses* 3.24.88, *Enchiridion* 3). The Stoic practice of *praemeditatio malorum:* contemplating possible misfortunes to prevent devastating grief.

181 Epictetus: "No one can rob us of our Moral Will": An axiom from *Discourses.*

182 Epictetus, *Discourses* 2.18.28. The "contest" (ἀγών) is the daily philosophical struggle over Assent and Judgment; the stakes are not external rewards but the integrity of the Ruling Faculty itself.

183 Epictetus quotations on assent, impulse, and "the contest": From Epictetus's *Discourses.* The three Stoic disciplines (assent, impulse, and desire) map onto Marcus's organizing framework throughout the *Meditations:* what to believe, how to act, what to want.

BOOK 12

184 Xylander reads προκειμένου σοι σωματίου ("the little body set before you"), where the modern text has περικειμένου ("the little body lying around you"). Xylander's own Latin, *corpori tibi circundato* ("the body placed around you"), follows the modern reading rather than his own Greek, suggesting he recognized the corruption or had access to a better reading. This translation follows the Xylander Latin.

185 Xylander reads ἐκ προπαθείας ("from pre-passion" or "from prior susceptibility"), where the modern text has ἐκ προσπαθείας ("from attachment"). The difference is a single letter: προ- ("before") versus προσ- ("toward"). The Xylander reading implies things that cling to the Ruling Faculty through an antecedent emotional vulnerability; the modern reading implies things that cling through acquired attachment. Xylander's Latin simply transliterates his Greek. This translation follows the modern reading as producing the clearer philosophical sense.

186 The sphere of Empedocles: Empedocles (c. 494-434 BCE) envisioned cosmic perfection as a self-contained Sphere, "rejoicing in its circular solitude." Marcus uses it as a model for the self-sufficient Psyche.
The quotation itself presents a textual variant: Xylander reads μονῇ περιγηθεῖ (*monē perigēthei,* "rejoicing in solitude"), where modern critical editions read μονίῃ περιηγέι (*moniē periēgei,* "revolving in solitude"), following Empedocles Fr. 28 (DK).
The translation combines elements of both readings: "rejoicing in its circular solitude."

187 Xylander reads εὐγενῶς ("nobly"), where the modern text has εὐμενῶς ("with goodwill" or "benevolently"). This translation follows the Xylander reading, rendered as "nobly," which in context captures the spirit of both variants.

188 Pancratiast (παγκρατιαστής): An athlete competing in the pancratium, a Greek combat sport combining wrestling and boxing.

189 The Xylander text gives no location for Lupus; the modern edition adds ἐν τοῖς κήποις ("in the gardens"). The name also varies: Xylander reads Λοῦπος (Lupus); the modern text reads Δοῦπος (Dupus).

190 A litany of men who retreated to luxurious estates, now forgotten. Tiberius at Capri is the emperor (r. 14-37 CE) who withdrew to his island villa in 26 CE and never returned to

Rome. Stertinius at Baiae evokes the fashionable resort on the Bay of Naples; Stertinius himself is otherwise unidentified. Fabius Catullinus, Lusius Lupus, and Velius Rufus are also unidentified.

191 The five-act structure was articulated as a rule for drama by Horace (*Ars Poetica* 189-190) and became the dominant framework through which Renaissance editors later organized the plays of Plautus and Terence, though the original Roman comedies were likely performed without formal act divisions. Marcus's actor-exit metaphor draws on this conventional framework, imagining Nature dismissing the actor after three. The praetor was the magistrate who organized public games and could end performances.